WILDLIFE OF THE CHANNEL ISLANDS

The Pink Sea Fan Eunicella verrucosa, *a delicate, slow-growing coral photographed in the clear waters around Sark.*

Wildlife of the Channel Islands

Sue Daly

Foreword by Lee Durrell

SEAFLOWER BOOKS

Published in 2004 by
SEAFLOWER BOOKS
1 The Shambles
Bradford on Avon
Wiltshire   BA15 1JS

Origination by Seaflower Books

Printed in Italy

ISBN 1 903341 24 8

© 2004 Sue Daly

CONTENTS

	Foreword by Lee Durrell	7
	Preface	9
	Introduction	11
1	Cliffs and Heaths	21
2	Reefs and Islets	41
3	Beaches and Dunes	63
4	Rocky Shores	87
5	Beneath the Waves	113
6	The Interiors	137
7	Seeing Wildlife in the Channel Islands	171
8	The Future	203
	Useful addresses and websites	209
	Bibliography	213
	Acknowledgements	215
	Index	217

View from Jersey's north coast

Foreword

The Channel Islands are a crossroads for wildlife. Geographically, we lie between northern and southern Europe, climatically, we are deeply affected by the Gulf Stream, and our natural history is a tapestry woven of those influences. The Islands are a stopover or seasonal home for migratory birds. Our human inhabitants are of many origins and have, through the ages, had multiple effects on our wild landscapes. The biodiversity of the Channel Islands is thus rich, varied and unique.

Sue Daly, known for her passionate interest in the Islands' marine life, has popped up above the surface and turned her keen eye and wit to things terrestrial. As with her films and other written work, Sue's treatment of wildlife is thoroughly researched, but her style is so charming and joyful that the reader is effortlessly attracted by and warmly welcomed into this fascinating corner of the natural world.

Wildlife of the Channel Islands does not purport to be an exhaustive account, but rather a guided tour through the habitats, land and sea, with lively commentary on what animals and plants are likely to be found and how they fit into the ecology of the Islands as a whole. We learn about orchids, butterflies and red squirrels, as well as congers and cows, gorse and *vraic*. Did you know there are no moles on Guernsey? What is special about the perfume of the sweet violet? Have you seen the amazing gannet colony off Alderney? Why are Jerseymen called *crapauds*? Don't you marvel at the little marine worms that move to the rhythm of the Islands' extraordinary tides, even if displaced far from home?

The Islands are also at a crossroads in time. We are facing decisions about governance and management at home and about relationships with institutions and countries beyond our shores. Directly or indirectly, swiftly or gradually, for better or for worse, the outcomes *will* affect our natural heritage. It is essential that we residents and our cherished visitors know about our wildlife communities so that we all understand the ramifications of changing or losing them.

I can think of no better introduction to the wildlife of the Channel Islands than this enchanting book.

Lee Durrell
Jersey
August 2004

Les Écréhous reef, half-way between north-east Jersey and the coast of Normandy, forms an extensive network of rocky outcrops and shallow lagoons. It is an important breeding site for several species of seabird.

Preface

The first time I came to the Channel Islands I fell instantly in love with them. It was early spring, the hedgerows were splashed yellow with daffodils, the first vivid green leaves were unfurling and the elegant Jersey Cows wore canvas jackets, protection against the still chilly wind. But what struck me most was the colour of the sea. Even at that time of year it was the most intense shade of blue I had ever seen.

Lured by this shimmering turquoise water I took up scuba diving and the love affair deepened, literally. I was utterly enchanted by the marine life that I encountered, from sapphire blue Lobsters and tiny purple-striped Anemone Prawns, to colour-changing Cuttlefish and enormous Conger Eels. Since then I have struggled to capture these wonderful creatures on film as a photographer and, more recently, a natural history film-maker.

So great was my passion for all things marine that for over ten years I barely noticed that the Channel Islands are also home to an unbelievable variety of 'non-fishy' wildlife. With blinkers now removed I am discovering that the flora and fauna of the land are every bit as captivating as those underwater. Who could fail to be impressed by whole fields of orchids or a glimpse of an emerald Green Lizard, for all the world like a miniature dragon, stalking its prey in the sand dunes? The sight of the ten-thousand-strong Gannet colony is surely one of Europe's greatest natural spectacles while the virtuoso performance of a Skylark accompanied by an orchestra of insects is a sound to cherish forever. Whether ambling along a flower-lined cliff path in spring or struggling against the wind on a deserted winter beach to the haunting calls of Curlew and Oystercatcher, these islands continue to fascinate me. I've learnt that the wildlife here is a startling blend of the common and the exotic and that no other place in Britain can claim a flora and fauna so rich. A marvellous mix of plants and animals from much further south thrive alongside those from northern Europe making this one of nature's most dramatic crossroads. The Islands are well known as a tourist destination and a centre of international finance, but I believe their real value lies in their remarkable natural history. Whether a visitor or resident, I hope you enjoy this book and treasure the wildlife of these beautiful islands.

Sue Daly
Jersey
2004

Introduction

Cradled in the bay of St Malo, the Channel Islands form an archipelago between the northern coast of Brittany and the western coast of Normandy. Although they swear allegiance to the English crown, they are geographically very much part of the Continent and that they are politically British and not French is simply an accident of history. Victor Hugo, who spent sixteen years in exile in Jersey and Guernsey, put it most succinctly when he described the islands as, 'pieces of France which fell into the sea and were gathered up by England'. In 1066 the Islands were part of the Duchy of Normandy when its leader, William the Conqueror, triumphed at the Battle of Hastings and became King of England. At the beginning of the thirteenth century the continental lands were lost to the Duchy but the Islands have remained part of the British Isles ever since. At times they have been separated by opposing loyalties such as in the seventeenth century when Guernsey supported Cromwell's rebellion and Jersey stayed loyal to the crown. Maybe such ancient differences account for the half-joking but friendly rivalry that still exists between the two largest islands.

The French influence, however, cannot be overestimated and is very much in evidence in the Islands' languages and the majority of their place names. Geologically the link is even stronger for the islands were once part of the Continent. By the end of the last ice age, some six thousand years ago, the English Channel had finally formed as sea levels gradually rose. Once a scattering of hills overlooking a vast plain, the rising water isolated some parts before others. Guernsey, Sark and Herm were the first to become islands. Alderney soon followed but Jersey maintained its connection with France much longer due to an extensive tundra-like plain that formed a land bridge to the Continent. Eventually this too was flooded and Jersey became an island. The 'bridge' still exists as a shallow underwater plateau around the south and east of the island. It has been calculated that if the tide were to fall by the same amount again as it does on the lowest spring tide Jersey would once again be joined to France.

Lying over a hundred miles south of the British mainland, Jersey is the largest and most southerly of the Channel Islands. Like all the others it is composed mainly of granite causing the soil to be mostly acidic except in the areas, sometimes extensive, where superficial deposits of calcium-rich seashells provide a haven for lime-loving plants. Measuring almost eleven miles by seven at its widest, it has a rugged cliff-lined north coast and slopes gently down to the south. Broad sandy bays are a feature of the east, west and south coasts with rocky headlands in-between. A series of deep wooded valleys run from north to south through the island's beautiful interior.

The Bailiwick of Guernsey is made up of the other four main Islands. Guernsey has its cliffs on the south and slopes down towards its northern end which is surrounded on both sides by sandy bays and inlets. Until the beginning of the nineteenth century it was two separate islands at high tide, Guernsey and the low lying island of Vale, joined by a bridge and a crossing at low water. In 1803 the gap between the two was filled in although the area where the sea once separated them is still called the Bridge.

Alderney, the most northerly island, is also the closest to France being just eight miles west of the Cotentin Peninsula. Measuring three and a half miles by less than two, it also has high cliffs on the south and a northern half that slopes gently down to the sea in a series of sweeping sandy bays. Being much more exposed it suffers stronger winds than the other Islands but, contrary to popular belief, is not entirely without trees having some small wooded valleys.

Jethou, the smallest permanently occupied island in the Channel Islands is privately owned but easily seen from the nearby Island of Herm.

Sark, nine miles east of Guernsey, is almost completely surrounded by steep cliffs. Some sandy beaches are uncovered as the tide drops and it is also home to one of the smallest harbours in the world. The top of the island is a fairly level plateau with some lushly-wooded valleys lining the cliff paths down to the sea. Three miles long and a mile and a half wide, the main island is connected to the smaller Little Sark by a dramatically narrow isthmus called La Coupée. Between Sark and Guernsey lies the

Introduction

tiny island of Herm. Owned by the States of Guernsey, it is leased to private tenants but they warmly welcome visitors. Although only a mile and a half long by less than a mile wide it has a magical mixture of cliffs, heathland, dunes and the famous Shell Beach. The only other islands that are permanently occupied are Brecqhou, off Sark, and Jethou, close to Herm, but both are privately owned and impossible to visit without an invitation. Lihou, the most westerly point in the Channel Islands, is an islet joined to Guernsey by a causeway at low water and is now managed as a nature reserve. Burhou, a low-lying island just north of Alderney, is also a protected area being home to the largest breeding colony of Puffins in the Islands.

As well as these main islands the archipelago is scattered with treacherous, half-submerged reefs that combine with the enormous tidal range to make the waters around the Channel Islands a mariner's nightmare. The Casquets Reef north-west of Alderney has claimed many victims despite the presence of a lighthouse. Les Minquiers Plateau, half way between Jersey and St Malo, is a vast area of rocky outcrops and shifting sand banks with a few small buildings on the main island used as summer retreats. Les Écréhous, off the north-east coast of Jersey, is a smaller reef and it too has a cluster of tiny homes. There are countless other smaller reefs, islets and stacks all named and carefully marked on the maritime charts of the area. The salt spray, summer drought and lashing winter storms mean that the number of plants in these areas is limited but, being relatively undisturbed, they make ideal nesting sites for sea birds.

When it comes to understanding the distribution of wildlife in the Channel Islands there are three main factors to take into account. The first is the difference in time between the islands being cut off from each other and from the Continent. Plant and animal species slowly advancing north-west across Europe were able to colonise Jersey for longer than they had to reach the other Islands. This, and its greater diversity of habitats, accounts for Jersey having the greatest variety of wildlife along with more Continental species than the other Islands. Quite when Jersey finally became an island is unknown but its

The Jersey Bank Vole Clethrionmys glareolus caesarius *is as much at home in woodlands and hedgebank as in the rough grasslands and Gorse of the coast. Like the Guernsey Short-tailed Field Vole it is sufficiently different from all other races to be considered a separate species (AC)*

separation stopped the natural spread of any terrestrial species that could not travel by air or sea. In evolutionary terms the six thousand or so years that the Islands have been isolated has been long enough to allow the emergence of several distinct island races. With a limited gene pool and the intervention of man, the Jersey and Guernsey cows are an extreme example but similar developments have taken place in the wild. The Long-tailed Field Mouse in the Islands is larger and more brightly coloured than its mainland counterpart. The Bank Vole in Jersey is sufficiently different from all other races to be considered a separate species as is Guernsey's Short-tailed Field Vole.

Other differences are less easy to explain. Guernsey, Alderney and Herm are home to the White-toothed Shrew, a slightly smaller version of that found on the Continent. Jersey and Sark have the Lesser White-toothed Shrew. It too is a Continental species, not found at all on the British mainland, but strangely absent from adjacent coastline of France as well. Alderney, for some reason, has no Magpies but does have plenty of Moles, unlike Guernsey which is mole free. The latter may be explained by the earlier separation of Guernsey from the Continent but quite why some disgruntled Jersey gardener with a grudge against his island neighbour has never 'introduced' any moles is harder to understand.

Sea fog, an occasional feature of Channel Island weather that shrouds the coast yet leaves the tops of the islands clear.

Introduction

The second influence on the wildlife of the Islands is the climate. Thousands of miles away shallow Caribbean seas are warmed by the tropical sun. The rotation of the earth, combined with the unfailing trade winds, pushes this water north and east across the Atlantic forming the Gulf Stream. The main flow sweeps along the western coasts of Ireland and Scotland while one portion is deflected eastwards past the Islands and along the Channel. The powerful current churns up essential nutrients from deeper water depositing them in the coastal shallows and enriching the Islands' marine life. It also has a warming influence on the climate ensuring mild oceanic weather with few severe frosts or snowfalls and sea temperatures that seldom fall below eight or ten degrees centigrade. At the other extreme, the tiny land mass of the Islands means that extremely high temperatures rarely have time to build up. Sea fog is an occasional feature of the weather eerily rolling up the cliffs yet leaving the tops of the Islands clear. More common is a dense belt of low fog which, even in summer, can cloak the area for days at a time closing the Islands' three airports.

Such a mild and equable climate means that many plants and animals that would perish at a similar latitude in Continental Europe can survive in the Channel Islands. Some Mediterranean species, such as the Jersey Thrift, are at the most northerly edge of their range and are not found on the other side of the Channel. Another flower, the tiny Sand Crocus, is widespread in the islands but much celebrated at the one location it is found in on the British mainland.

Discarded garden plants, such as *Carpobrotus*, that would perish just a little further north often thrive in the

Giant Echium Echium pininana *or Rocket Plant, one of the many garden escapes originally from much further south that survive wild in the Channel Islands because of the mile climate and the lack of severe frosts. Growing over four metres tall, it attracts so many bees that it's also known locally as the Bee Plant*

wild, sometimes at the cost of the native plants, with little or no frost to kill them off in winter. The Agile Frog and Green Lizard are yet more examples of Continental species living here but no further north giving the Channel Islands' wildlife a slightly exotic flavour.

The prevailing wind plays a key role in the distribution of wildlife in the Channel Islands. Species that cannot tolerate the desiccation and salt that it brings must live far inland, an impossibility on some of the smaller islands and reefs.

Yet there is one major aspect of the weather in the Islands that is often less than favourable; the prevailing south-westerly wind. Blowing straight in from the Atlantic it can bring gales that last for well over a week and lash salt spray far inland. For the plants, and particularly the trees, this can make life difficult and only those tolerant of the salt-laden winds can survive in the most exposed areas. For the lichen this wind is essential, bringing with it, as it does, clean air straight from the Atlantic. A symbiotic association of an alga and a fungus, lichen will not tolerate a polluted atmosphere and the huge areas of rock, roof and building that it covers are a welcome sign of the Islands' excellent air quality. Occasionally the predominately mild climate is interrupted by extremes of weather. The summers of 1976 and 1983 bought heat-wave and drought while the Great Storm of 1987 wreaked havoc and destroyed many mature trees. The winter of 1962/3 was exceptionally cold, freezing the reservoirs and even the edge of the sea in places. Conger Eels were found frozen solid on the shore and the Octopus, once abundant in shallow rocky areas, has only very occassionally been seen since.

The final, and perhaps greatest, influence on the wildlife of the Channel Islands is man. The stacked remains of Woolly Rhinoceroses and Mammoths in a cave in Jersey suggest that early forms of humans were hunting these animals on the plain that existed between the Islands and France over a hundred thousand years ago. Fifty thousand years or so later Neanderthal man arrived but, as a hunter and gatherer of wild fruit and berries, he is unlikely to have made much impact on the wildlife. A mere five thousand years ago Neolithic man colonised the Islands, living for the first

Introduction

Sea Ivory Ramalina siliquosa *one of more than three hundred species of lichen that thrive in the unpolluted atmosphere of the Channel Islands.*

time in settled communities and developing the earliest farming techniques. The native forests of Oak, Alder and Hazel were cleared for his animals and crops and man has been changing the Islands to suit his needs, with increasing momentum, ever since.

Over the centuries the Channel Islanders have adapted their agricultural activities to suit economic conditions. Historical documents from the twelfth and thirteenth centuries report that most of the fertile land was used to grow corn and that trees were so scarce that wood to repair the castles had to be imported from England. Rabbits, introduced for their meat in the Middle Ages, soon escaped from their warrens and further restricted the growth of tree seedlings throughout the Islands with their constant grazing. In the absence of wood, Gorse and dried seaweed were used as fuel. From Elizabethan times onwards much of the common land was gradually enclosed and seaweed was used to maintain the fertility of the thin, often sandy, soil that was continuously cultivated. From the sixteenth to the end of the nineteenth century cider apples were much in demand

Many plants and animals have been introduced, intentionally or otherwise, by man. The seeds of Corn Marigold Chrysanthemum segetum *are thought to have arrived with the seeds of agricultural crops.*

17

and great swathes of arable land in Jersey and Guernsey were planted with orchards. Huge walls were built to shelter the trees from the wind and their remains, along with circular granite apple crushers, still add character to the islands.

Many of the plants now living wild in the Channel Islands were initially introduced by man. Some, such as the Three-cornered Leek, were brought over deliberately. Originally a garden plant, it is now well established in the wild and its pungent white flowers line many lanes and footpaths in the early spring. The Hottentot Fig, common on the cliffs, was originally found around some of the Islands' forts which may indicate that it was inadvertently introduced by the Victorian armies who built them. Other plants have accidentally stowed away on ships in packaging or goods from foreign lands or hitched lifts as seeds attached to the clothing of travellers. The bulbs of the Guernsey Lily, a native of South Africa, were thought to have washed ashore from a ship wrecked on the island's coast during a storm. A slightly different version of the bulbs' arrival tells of a ship en route from Cape Horn which grounded off Guernsey in the 1650s. A local landowner who helped refloat the vessel was rewarded by the crew with a gift of the exotic bulbs.

If the wind is blowing in the right direction on a summer's day it can deliver a real wildlife treasure, the Swallowtail Butterfly Papilio machaon. *This occasional Continental visitor adds a distinctly exotic flavour to the wildlife of the Channel Islands (RP)*

Whether native or introduced, the wildlife of the Channel Islands remains a fascinating mixture of the common and the unusual. Each island and islet has its own unique blend of flora and fauna with a few species not found in the others. They are a botanist's paradise with around eighteen hundred plant species in just over seventy-

Introduction

five square miles, three or four times the level of diversity of a comparable area on the British mainland. The nearby Normandy coast forms a 'funnel' for migrating birds during the spring and autumn offering excellent opportunities for sightings of the more than three hundred species of birds recorded in the Islands. Add to these the vast amount of other flying, crawling or swimming animals that live, or spend at least some of their time, in the Channel Islands and it makes an attempt to include them all in one book all but impossible. Instead this book is intended to give the briefest guide to some of the most common plants and animals that live here along with those that make the Islands different from each other and from the mainlands of France and Britain between which they lie. The aim therefore is to whet the wildlife appetite. Rather than describe each group of the flora and fauna separately, I have chosen instead to look at the different types of habitats in the Islands and the wildlife likely to be found in each. This is, after all, how we encounter the natural world. There is obviously a certain amount of overlap between the chapters as habitats often merge gradually into each other and some plants and animals can be found in more than one specific environment. Oystercatchers, for example, feed on both sandy beaches and rocky shores and Kestrels can be found hunting over just about any part of the Islands. A comprehensive guide to all the Islands' wildlife would be the life's work of several people. Many excellent volumes on specific areas or aspects of local natural history already exist and are listed in the bibliography for those who want to delve more deeply into the treasure trove that is the wildlife of the Channel Islands.

Early summer on the cliff tops of Alderney and the wildflowers provide a natural display more stunning than any garden. The parasitic Greater Broomrape Orobanche rapum-genistae (in the foreground) flowers in June and July but its dry flower spikes often persist for many months afterwards (AC).

Chapter One

Cliffs and Heaths

Exposed to the full force of the Atlantic Ocean and the prevailing south-westerly wind, the cliffs of the Channel Islands would appear to be the least hospitable environment for any form of wildlife. The autumn and winter gales pound the granite heights drenching all in their path and sending salt-laden spray far inland. In summer the sun bakes the rocks and headlands relentlessly and combines with the wind to dry everything to a crisp. And yet the miles of sheer cliffs and rock strewn heaths are home to an impressive variety of wildlife, all of which thrive in this turbulent realm between land and sea.

Right: Sea Campion Silene vulgaris *ssp.* uniflora *flowers almost all year round in the Channel Islands but, like many plants on the cliffs, is at its best in early summer. In Jersey French it has five names, three of which refer to a child's game where the calyx is turned inside out and the petals removed to reveal a figure like a lady in a crinoline dress.*

Left: Thrift Armeria maritima *can cope with a regular drenching in salt water and so thrives close to the water line along with the orange lichen* Xanthoria parietina.

Wildlife of the Channel Islands

Much of the Channel Islands' coasts are naturally fortified by steep granite cliffs with some reaching almost ninety metres above sea level. At the base of the cliffs, washed by waves even on the calmest days, are two bands of colour formed by lichen neither of which have a common name. The lower is a matt black encrustation called *Verrucaria maura* sometimes mistaken for a layer of oil or tar. Above that are dense patches of orangey-yellow *Xanthoria parietina*, a species also found on walls and rock faces inland. The first of the flowering plants are able to grow in this splash zone wherever they can find enough of a crevice or hollow to gain a foothold. Thrift has a very long, branching tap root to both hold it in place and seek out to tiniest traces of water. Its upper leaves form a dense mat that shelter those beneath and from April onwards drifts of pom-pom-headed flowers paint patches of even the steepest cliff face pale pink. Interestingly the Jersey Thrift, a Mediterranean species which blooms later, cannot cope with salt-water downpours and flowers further inland. Rock Samphire and Sea Beet, both edible plants, can survive this close to the sea but develop thicker, more leathery, leaves when growing on the cliffs than they do in more sheltered areas. No doubt this helps the plants retain more of their precious moisture on the weather-blasted cliffs. It is no coincidence that many of the other plants that carpet the lower, salt-lashed regions of the cliffs have 'sea' in their name. Sea Plantain, Sea Spurrey and Sea Campion all grow where their roots can find the tiniest toehold with the last forming thick cushions of creamy-white flowers that are at their best in late spring. This is the peak flowering season for most of the cliff-dwelling plants before the full heat of the summer sun parches what little soil there is. Sea Spleenwort, the only truly maritime fern, prefers a little more shade and grows in small caves and beneath overhanging rocks, its fine fronds reaching up to two feet in length.

One of the most striking plants on the cliffs around the Islands is also the least popular with local botanists. The Hottentot Fig has thick, fleshy, triangular leaves that

Beautiful but not entirely welcome. The Hottentot Fig Carpobrotus *sp. may add a vivid splash of colour to the cliffs around the Channel Islands but at what cost to the native vegetation?*

22

Cliffs and Heaths

are ideally suited to the heat of its native South Africa. A popular garden plant, it began appearing in the wild at the turn of the last century and is destroyed only by the severest of frosts, a rarity in the Channel Islands. Although its edible fruit rarely ripens this far north, the plant is more than able to propagate itself without producing seeds using instead its rapidly growing roots and stems. It forms dense, heavy carpets which drape the cliffs with vivid pink and yellow flowers, smothering the less vigorous native plants. Often its sheer weight brings down whole sections of rock and soil which are washed away, along with the plant, on the highest tides. Herring Gulls are also blamed for its spread by using apparently lifeless pieces of the plant's stem as nesting material. In the guano-rich environment around the nest such 'cuttings' take root easily and so the suffocating plant is distributed to the remotest stacks and islets. Remarkably Sark continues to be free from the Hottentot Fig even though it is now creeping along the coast of nearby Herm.

Less able to tolerate salt water than some of the other plants on the cliffs, Sheep's-bit Jasione motana *grows above the splash zone.*

Bluebells Hyacinthoides non-scripta *are a common feature on many of the Islands' coasts but are particularly abundant on the cliffs of Sark.*

Wildlife of the Channel Islands

Higher up the cliffs the vegetation becomes more varied as the salt-loving plants are joined by those a little less tolerant to sea water. Pennywort, Bird's-foot Trefoil, Sheep's-bit, Rock Sea-lavender, English Stonecrop and Ox-eye Daisy all add their colours to the tapestry of rock face and ledge. Where enough soil has accumulated to protect their bulbs in hollows and hanging valleys, Bluebells grow in great profusion. In late spring great swathes of the Islands' coasts are painted with a vivid purple-blue haze as their flowers bloom on the cliffs. More often associated with woodlands, they survive here only because of the Bracken which grows up as their flowers fade, shading the bulbs that would otherwise perish in such an exposed environment. The tiny island of Burhou is also carpeted in Bluebells in spring but for some reason it is the garden variety known as the Spanish Bluebell that thrives here and on much of nearby Alderney. Later on in the year the Bluebells benefit from the Bracken again when it dies back and enriches the impoverished soil. These bulbs though are probably the only plants to benefit from Bracken for it spreads rapidly and little else can survive in its shade. Its stems run deep underground making it difficult to remove and even the occasional bush fires that flare up on the cliffs in summer have little long term effect on the plant's progress. In the past it was a valuable commodity which, when cut and dried, was used as fuel and for animal bedding. In the most rural areas it formed the filling of day-beds in autumn and winter for the Islands' knitters, but both practices had died out by the First World War. Known to cause cancer in animals, it is rarely used now for bedding. It is a pity that no modern application can be found for Bracken as it continues to flourish in all of the Islands often at the expense of less vigorous plants.

Less than ten millimetres across, the Sand Crocus Romulea columnae *flourishes on the Channel Islands' cliff tops and in other areas of sandy turf but is found at only one site on the British mainland. It blooms on sunny days in early spring but finding it often means resorting to hands and knees.*

Cliffs and Heaths

Like all members of its family, the Spotted Rock-rose Tuberaria guttata *opens briefly in the morning sun but sheds its petals by early afternoon. It flowers from early June for a few weeks but does not bloom at all on cloudy days.*

At the top of the cliffs, in areas where the larger vegetation is kept in check by the constantly grazing rabbits, a thorough search of the springy moss and turf may reveal a real gem of a flower. The minute Sand Crocus is no larger than a well-bitten little fingernail and only flowers on the sunniest days in March and April. A real rarity on mainland Britain, its pale purple or white flowers are not uncommon in the Islands but, because of its size, go unnoticed by all but the sharpest-eyed botanists. Another warmth-loving plant well worth looking for is the Spotted Rock-rose which blooms a few weeks later in early June. Its pale yellow petals are marked with a red-brown spot near the base and remain closed in dull or rainy weather. Even on sunny days it proves an elusive quarry for around midday its petals wilt and fall to the ground.

Prostrate Broom Cytisus scoparius *ssp.* maritimus *has adapted to life on the weather-blasted cliffs by growing close to the rock face rather than forming an upright shrub. Genetically different from the ordinary Broom, it thrives on the south-western cliffs of Jersey, Guernsey and Alderney.*

Dodder Cuscuta epithymum *is a parasite gaining all its nutrients from its host plant. Without any need for them, its leaves are reduced to tiny, inconspicuous scales. In the past farmers in Guernsey used to wrap a handful of dodder in a fresh cabbage leaf to treat some ailments in their cattle.*

Much easier to find is the Prostrate Broom, another yellow-flowered plant that favours the cliff tops. As its name suggests, it grows flat against the ground or rock face and continues to do so even if moved to a more sheltered location. This characteristic has evolved to cope with the almost constant wind and it has developed as a completely separate subspecies the seedlings of which also remain flat. In Jersey and Alderney it is often host to a parasitic plant called Greater Broomrape which grows from the roots of the Broom tapping directly into the larger plant's supply of nutrients. With no need of chlorophyll, the green substance which plants use to produce food from the sun, Broomrape is almost colourless and produces no leaves of its own, just an upright flower-covered stem (illustrated on page 20). The cliff tops are also home to another parasitic plant, Dodder. Its thread-like orange stems grow in a tangled web so dense that it can completely engulf other vegetation. In July it produces a mass of tiny, spherical pink flowers with a powerful, honey-like scent. When its seed germinates it immediately sends out an exploratory shoot that entwines itself around the nearest plant. A sucker penetrates the stem and, once secure, the root of the Dodder withers and dies as it begins to feed directly on the unfortunate host. It can grow on a wide variety of plants, particularly those in the pea and heather families, and in the Islands is most conspicuous on Gorse, the commonest shrub on the cliff tops.

Also known as Furze, Gorse played an important role in the rural economy of the Channel Islands for centuries. With few trees and no coal it was greatly valued by the Islanders as a fuel to power the huge bread ovens that were built into the fireplace of every farmhouse. Also used as fodder for horses, it was cut back every three years and strict regulations were drawn up to govern its harvest with heavy penalties imposed on those who breached them. There is an Island saying that kissing is out of fashion when the Gorse is out of bloom, a reference to the fact that, this far south, it flowers pretty much all year round. Guernsey folklore reinforces this with the tale of a man on

Gorse Ulex europaeus *with Fort Raz and the treacherous Alderney race in the background. Although it blooms all year round, Gorse flowers are at their peak in early spring when they release a heady coconut-scented perfume. On windless late summer days the sharp cracking noise of the pods exploding and scattering the seeds can be heard clearly.*

Named after the area in southern England where it was originally described, the Dartford Warbler Sylvia undata *needs dense cover and mild winters to survive (MD).*

his deathbed who made his wife promise not to remarry while there were still flowers on the Gorse. It has long been thought to ward off evil spirits and some builders still place a spring in the chimney of homes they complete. Now no longer harvested, much of the spiky shrub is left to smother great areas of cliff top where it grows leggy and clogged with old wood. It burns readily and a piece of broken glass or carelessly dropped cigarette end can reduce huge areas of headland scrub to ash and charcoal. Such fires are common but, although they appear very destructive, actually cause little long term damage and may even be of benefit to the overall environment. The fire spreads rapidly through the dry vegetation but usually passes quickly leaving the roots undamaged and animals sheltering underground are often unharmed. When Gorse regrows it forms a far denser thicket than the old shrubs providing much better cover for wildlife, particularly the birds, that rely on it.

The best known of these is the Dartford Warbler, a Mediterranean species which is one of the islands' most treasured breeding birds, and one of the rarest. Although their nests are destroyed by the cliff top fires they seem happy to relocate and are far more susceptible to cold winters, fortunately rare in the Islands, which deprive them of their diet of insects and spiders. Secretive and shy, ornithologists describe the Dartfords' habit of flitting among the low shrubs as 'skulking', a slightly dowdy term for such an attractive bird. Both sexes are dark in colour and easily distinguished from other small heathland birds by their long tails which are constantly cocked and flicked. The male has a rich, ruddy-brown breast and is most easily observed in April, the breeding season, when he delivers his scratchy call either from the top of a Gorse-bush or during his elegant song flight. He builds a series of flimsy nests, presumably to impress his mate, but the real nest is mostly the work of the female bird. It consists of a deep cup of grass and roots built close to the ground and interwoven with moss and spiders' silk. The three or four eggs hatch in just twelve days and the young fledge less than a month later leaving the parents time to produce a second and, sometimes, even a third brood in the same year. Being able to reproduce in such relatively large numbers is essential for a bird whose population can be almost wiped out in a few days of cold winter weather.

The mixture of Gorse and rough grassland on the Islands' heaths provides a perfect home for many other species of bird. Flocks of Linnets swirl from one feeding site to another, twittering their musical song as they go. From a distance they appear dull and unremarkable but the male's breeding plumage is an elegant contrast of russet and pale grey with a rosy-crimson breast and crown. In spring Whitethroats return to the Channel Islands chirping their scratchy song from the tangled undergrowth where they breed. The Stonechat has an even more distinctive call which can best be described as sounding like two pebbles chinking together. This must surely be the origin of its onomatopoeic Guernsey French name of *Crax*. Some spend the winter here but most arrive in spring to breed. The male is a handsome bird with a black head, rust-coloured breast and contrasting white collar and is easily seen proclaiming his territory from the top of a Gorse bush. Less conspicuous is the Meadow Pipit, a small brown bird with a squeaky song flight that often ends in a musical trill as it 'parachutes' to the ground. But the greatest vocal performer of them all is another insignificant-looking bird; the Skylark. It delivers its song from so high up in the sky that the bird is virtually invisible as it pours forth its burbling, liquid harmonies. Ironically some of the best places to appreciate the song of the Skylark is at the Islands' airports where its warbling melody is discernible between the roar of engines. Like many of the heathland birds it nests on the ground concealed in a tussock of grass and starts breeding early in the season. The four or five chicks fledge relatively quickly so that a second and sometimes even a third brood can be reared. For ground-nesting birds whose young are so vulnerable to predation, this breeding strategy is essential and contrasts with many of the seabirds who raise just one chick a year.

Hidden in the grass the chicks of the Skylark Alauda arvensis *must remain silent and well camouflaged to survive the first few weeks of their life. In recent years their numbers in the Channel Islands have fallen dramatically but now seem to be slowly and steadily on the increase.*

The migration period of the Wheatear Oenanthe oenanthe *is fairly drawn out in both spring and autumn so they are seen in the Islands for several months. A few have bred here, often in disused rabbit holes, but most prefer to head further north (MD).*

Wildlife of the Channel Islands

Sometimes called Peewits because of their call, flocks of Lapwings Vanellus vanellus *are a common sight in open areas in the winter. They seem particularly fond of the fields at Guernsey airport (MD).*

Open grassy areas, particularly those close to the cliff tops, are an ideal stopping-off ground for migrating birds. Both spring and autumn see the regular appearance of Whinchats and Common and Black Redstarts. Local flocks of Linnets are swollen with migrants and the lucky birdwatcher may even glimpse a Ring Ouzel or exotic Golden Oriole. One of the earliest spring migrants is the Wheatear, a handsome member of the thrush family. In the breeding season the male's plumage is an attractive mixture of blue-grey and black with an apricot-coloured throat. In flight the white patch on the rump is revealed earning it the original title of 'white arse' from which its more polite common name is derived. Mixed flocks of Fieldfares and Redwings also take advantage of the Channel Islands as a refuelling point, stopping off between their winter feeding grounds further south and the Arctic where they breed. The Lapwing is another common migrant and many spend the whole winter in the Channel Islands flocking together in fields and open places. In recent years a few pairs have bred in Jersey beginning their courtship with an elaborate display by the male. He rises into the air slowly then twists and tumbles towards the ground as if out of control before pulling up at the last minute. These aerobatics are accompanied by a haunting medley of harsh, shrill calls. The eggs are laid in a simple scrape and the parents are known to struggle along the ground feigning injury if disturbed to lure a predator away from the nest. As soon as the final chick hatches they all flee the nest and head for the nearest cover. Speckled black and brown with a white collar and chest, the chicks feed themselves while their parents stand guard.

Top left: Bell Heather Erica cinerea *thrives on the cliff tops and heaths of the Channel Islands forming dense carpets of vivid purple from July to September. Here it is photographed on the north coast of Sark with the private island of Brecqhou visible in the distance.*

Top right: The leaves and stem of Jersey Cudweed Gnaphalium luteoalbum *are covered in a down of fine silver-grey hairs. It grows in sandy soil that is wet through the winter but dries out in the summer (RL).*

Left: Purple Viper's-bugloss Echium plantagineum *grew in such profusion in Jersey that it is often still known as Jersey Viper's-bugloss. The flattened stem of the plant at the back is the result of an unusual local growth form called fasciation.*

Wildlife of the Channel Islands

The acidic, sandy soil and exposed conditions of the cliff tops and heaths are also home to a colourful profusion of wildflowers. Many are commonly found on the British mainland but a few that thrive in the Channel Islands are absent or extremely rare any further north. In some years whole fields close to the cliffs on the south-west coast of Jersey are swamped with Purple Viper's Bugloss and it also grows further inland. In each colony a number of plants show an unusual growth form called fasciation whereby the normally round stems become flattened and incredibly wide. At up to almost a foot (30cm) across and with flowers blooming all along the edges this distortion gives the plant a cactus-like appearance. The connection with vipers relates to an ancient fanciful notion that the ripe seeds resemble a snake's head and recalls a time when it was used as a cure for snake bites. Interestingly Purple Viper's-bugloss is found only in Jersey yet the 'ordinary' species of Viper's Bugloss grows happily in Herm and Alderney but shuns the two larger islands, another example of the occasionally bizarre distribution of local plants and animals.

Another plant with a strong connection to the Channel Islands is Jersey Cudweed. First recorded as long ago as the 1680s, it appears sporadically in Jersey and the other Islands. It is known as Jersey Cudweed as far afield as Australia and South Africa. Like all cudweeds, it was once thought by farmers to aid the digestion of cattle, hence its name.

The bold stripes on the female Wasp Spider Argiope bruennichi *are presumably to warn off the birds that might otherwise eat her. The characteristic zigzag ribbon of silk in her radiating web is clearly visible (RP).*

Cliffs and Heaths

For those with a sharp eye and an interest in small creatures, the heathlands make a good hunting ground. A radiating spider's web built close to the ground among tussocks of grass may well be the work of the female Wasp Spider. Her legs and abdomen are beautifully striped in black, cream and pale yellow. The male, in comparison, is a dull brown dwarf about a third of her size. With her flask-shaped egg case nearby, the female hangs upside down in the web waiting for an insect to land in her sticky trap. Once snared she bundles her prey in silk to immobilise it while she injects a powerful digestive enzyme. This dissolves the tissues of the unfortunate insect to a liquid that the spider is then able to suck out like soup. Mating for these spiders can also be a grizzly affair. The tiny male approaches his mate cautiously and may even be encouraged by a rhythmic swinging motion of her body. He creeps beneath her and, as they mate, she slowly draws silk from her spinnerets and wraps it around him. Once the mating is over the male has to struggle free of his bonds if he is to survive. The first time he usually escapes with the loss of just a leg or two but males that live to mate a second time are normally not so lucky and end their lives as the female's dinner. A southern European species that seems to be gradually spreading north, the Wasp Spider was first recorded in the Channel Islands in the 1950s and has since been found in southern parts of England.

The Scilly Bee Bombus muscorum scyllionus *is a distinct subspecies of moss carder bumble bee found only in the Isles of Scilly and the Channel Islands.*

The cliff top flowers and shrubs also attract several species of bee and a carpet of purple Bell Heather in full bloom is the perfect place to sit and watch these industrious little creatures at work. A small bumble bee with pale yellow fur on its body, a gingery-brown head and black underparts is likely to be another local speciality, the Scilly Bee. Named after the Isles of Scilly where it was first found, it has since been discovered living in the Channel Islands. Like all bumble bees, it is relatively heavy so its body is packed with muscles to power its broad wings. Early in the morning the wings are vibrated to generate the heat the bee needs for flying and the thick layer of fur retains this warmth, even on the chilliest days. But life for a Scilly Bee, as for other bumble bees, is short and as autumn draws to an end it dies leaving a queen to hibernate through the winter and form a new colony in the spring.

The Green Hairstreak Callophrys rubi *spends much of its life chasing away rivals and establishing a territory. Its metallic green sheen, unique among British butterflies, is not a pigment colour but is formed by the effect of light reflecting off the microscopic scales which cover the wings.*

An iridescent blue butterfly on the heathlands of Sark may be the rare Silver-studded Blue Plebejus argus. *The row of silver spots that give it its name can only be seen when the butterfly settles and reveals its underwing (RL).*

The most dazzling of all the insects are the butterflies and almost fifty species have been recorded in the Islands. Some of these are accidental arrivals blown off course by adverse weather and seen only once or twice but, of those found here regularly, many can be seen on the heaths and cliff tops. The Green Hairstreak, Meadow Brown, Red Admiral, Common Blue and Gatekeeper are just some of those common throughout the summer. In May and June they are joined by the remarkable Painted Lady which migrates some eight hundred miles from North Africa. A closer look at

Cliffs and Heaths

The Glanville Fritillary Melitaea cinxia *is a real rarity in Britain now found only on the Isle of Wight. It flies in early May and through June and can be seen on the coasts of Alderney, Guernsey and Sark and occasionally in the other Islands.*

some of the more familiar butterflies may reveal a real rarity. The Common Blue, for example, can easily be mistaken for a Silver-studded Blue, a species whose numbers are rapidly diminishing in Britain along with its favoured heathland habitat. Its caterpillars have an unusual relationship with ants which they attract by releasing a sugary solution from a 'honey-gland' on their body. The ants feed on this sweet secretion and in return protect the caterpillars from predators and even move them to their food plants of Gorse, Broom and Heather. Even rarer still is the Glanville Fritillary, an eye-catching orange butterfly with dark brown checks and spots and tiny white squares edging the wings. Named after Eleanor Glanville, an enthusiastic eighteenth century collector, this sun-loving butterfly glides low over rough grassy slopes near the sea, stopping to drink nectar from yellow flowers such as Vetch and Trefoil. The eggs are laid on Plantains and hatch three weeks later. The black, bristly caterpillars spend the summer feeding and hibernate through the winter in a silken web until spring. In April each caterpillar transforms into a chrysalis and a month later the next generation of these precious butterflies emerge.

Despite its name the Jersey Tiger Moth Euplagia quadripuntaria *is found in all of the other Channel Islands and at a few sites in southern England but is most abundant around the Mediterranean.*

The boldest-coloured wings of all belong not to a butterfly but a day-flying moth, the Jersey Tiger. Its contrasting shades and prominent patterns startle predators and warn of its unpalatable taste. It feeds on nectar and can easily be distinguished from similar tiger moths by its cream-coloured stripes where the others have spots. At rest the delta-shaped wings are folded but in flight the hindwings are revealed; a flickering flash of orange or yellow.

The only snake in the Channel Islands, the Grass Snake Natrix natrix, *just lives in Jersey. Having no venom it is harmless to humans but does release a very unpleasant odour when frightened or handled roughly.*

The Slow Worm Anguis fragilis *is actually a legless lizard which feeds mostly on slugs ensuring it a welcome in any garden. Long-lived, Slow Worms have been known to survive for over fifty years in captivity.*

Of the four species of reptile living in the Channel Islands two live mostly on heathland but both are secretive and a quick glimpse of scaly skin disappearing through the undergrowth is all that is often seen of either. The largest is the Grass Snake which can grow over three feet (100cm) long and, of all the Islands, is only found in Jersey. It feeds on frogs, toads, small mammals and even nestling birds. An excellent swimmer, it will also take tadpoles, newts and fish. Like all snakes it uses its forked tongue to 'taste' the air and ground. The young Grass Snake has a distinct creamy-white collar which fades then disappears as it ages, a characteristic the Grass Snake in Jersey shares with a variety found much further south in Spain and Cyprus. Often mistaken for a snake, the Slow Worm is much paler in colour with fine silvery-bronze

Cliffs and Heaths

scales giving it a polished, metallic appearance. It is, in fact, a legless lizard and the remnants of limb stumps can be felt if you gently run your fingers along the animal's body. In common with lizards, and in contrast to snakes, it has closable eyelids and a fragile tail that is shed should the animal be grasped by it. Found on the three largest Islands, the Slow Worm rests by day in a hole under a stone or pile of leaves, emerging after dark or on dull rainy days to feed. The male is a uniform colour and often has pale blue spots on his sides. The female has darker flanks. She gives birth to a dozen or more live young which are patterned with striking gold and black stripes running the length of their bodies.

The Kestrel Falco tinnunculus *eats about one fifth of its body weight each day and the undigested bones, feather, fur and beetle wings in its pellets reveal much about its diet (MD).*

The Peregrine Falcon Falco peregrinus *stands at the top of the avian food chain and its mere presence is guaranteed to cause uproar and alarm among any flock of birds (MD).*

The reptiles are wise to keep out of sight for a Slow Worm or young Grass Snake would make an easy meal for the Islands' most common bird of prey, the Kestrel. Easily recognised by its rich chestnut colour and, in the male, the blue-grey tail and head, the Kestrel relies on excellent eyesight to catch its prey. It hunts over cliffs, open ground and hedgerows and its characteristic hover reveals the bird's total mastery of the air. Even on the most blustery day, as its wings beat rapidly and the tail is splayed, its head stays absolutely motionless as if fixed to the sky. From high up the large, sensitive eyes scan the ground for the slightest tell-tale movement. Once its prey is spied the Kestrel plunges down in a sudden swoop and grasps its meal with outstretched talons. If no food is spotted it moves on a little way and takes up the beautifully controlled hover again. The Kestrel's varied diet may be the key to its success along with its flexible attitude to nest sites. Most breed on the cliffs but others seem just as content in old trees and some even take advantage of the boxes put up for Barn Owls. In contrast, the Peregrine Falcon breeds only on the Islands' cliffs and in very small numbers. Yet the fact that this magnificent bird is gracing our coasts is something to be celebrated considering the centuries of abuse it has suffered from mankind. Prized above all the raptors, the Peregrine was the falconer's most treasured hunting bird and only earls, princes and kings were allowed to fly them. The invention of the shotgun in the eighteenth-century saw the demise of the hunting bird and the Peregrine, with its taste for fresh bird flesh, was persecuted by gamekeepers. Pigeon fanciers too destroyed the birds and their nests and the Victorians, with their passion for collecting stuffed birds and their eggs, took their toll on the Peregrine population. In the Second World War, when homing pigeons brought messages between occupied Europe and England, the Peregrine came in direct conflict with the military for pigeons are its very favourite food. Once again nests and birds were destroyed and on the south coast of England the Peregrine was just about wiped out. In the peace that followed numbers gradually recovered but plummeted again in the 1960s. Many birds failed to produce eggs and those that were laid were infertile or had shells so thin that they broke in the nest. The problems were eventually linked to the increased use of organochlorine pesticides which travel up the food chain from the land through the insects and birds and accumulate in the top predators which feed on them.

In the Channel Islands, where such pesticides were heavily used, both the Sparrowhawk and Peregrine were lost as breeding species although, interestingly, the Kestrel survived. Since then the most powerful chemicals have been banned and the birds of prey are making a welcome comeback. A pair of Peregrines now breed on each of the four largest Islands and recently second pairs, presumably their offspring, have been attempting to follow suit. Courtship involves a spectacular aerial display with high speed soaring and plunges accompanied by shrill calls as the pair engage talons in mid air. The male, called the tiercel, brings his mate gifts of food, an act

Cliffs and Heaths

thought to reinforce their bond and overcome the much larger female's natural aggression. The nest is a simple cliff ledge or crevice and the three or four eggs are laid at the beginning of April. Covered in fluffy white down for the first few days of their life, the chicks' flight feathers begin to form after twenty-one days. Two weeks later the young leave the nest but remain close by while their parents bring food and teach them the breathtaking hunting technique that is the Peregrine's trademark. With a territory of some four miles of cliff, they will take any bird from the tiny Goldcrest to Crows and seabirds striking a fatal blow in mid-air with dazzling speed and accuracy. Its spectacular near vertical stoop, with wings held back almost closed, reaches speeds of over a hundred miles an hour making it a raider of the skies without equal. The sight of a Peregrine effortlessly gliding the updrafts of a the windswept cliff is one of the most wonderful views in the Channel Islands, and long may it continue.

In early spring the footpaths above the cliffs of Herm are lined with breathtaking display of primroses, Primula vulgaris.

Les Minquiers Reef, the most southerly point of the Channel Islands. At high water there appears to be little more than a cluster of rocks but low water reveals almost forty square miles (100 sq km) of reef and sandbank.

Chapter Two

Reefs and Islets

The lighthouse on the Casquets marks the north-westerly point of an extensive reef reaching out from the coast of Alderney that includes Ortac, the Nannels and the island of Burhou.

A quick glance at a nautical chart of the Channel Islands is enough to strike terror in the heart of even the most experienced sailor, for the seas around the five main Islands are strewn with reefs and islets. Some are towering pinnacles rising sheer from the seabed while others form low lying outcrops and sandbanks that multiply in size as the tide falls. The smaller ones are swamped by the waves which wash away any signs of terrestrial life before it can settle while others are large enough to sport huts and cottages used by the Islanders as summer retreats. The flora and fauna of these reefs and rock stacks is less varied than that on the larger Islands but their comparative lack of human disturbance means that they often harbour some real wildlife treasures. The remotest is the Casquets Reef off the north-west coast of Alderney. Lying in the centre of the shipping lane between England and Guernsey, it has been the scene of many nautical tragedies. The first lighthouse was built there in 1724 and from then on some form of light was manned on the reef continuously until the end of the twentieth century when it was automated. People rarely land on the rocks now, leaving the gulls and Shags that breed there in peace. With sparse vegetation there is little to attract any other birds for any length of time although the keepers did make a considerable list of those that stopped there overnight, presumably migrants attracted by the lights and taking a much needed rest.

Less than two hundred yards from the shore, the Gannet colony on the Garden Rocks, also known as Les Étacs or Les Gardiens, is a breath-taking sight from the cliffs of Alderney. When the wind is in the right direction the constant sound, and the smell, are equally impressive.

A little further to the south-east there is a far busier scene, one which can only be described as the most stunning wildlife spectacle in the Channel Islands. Early in 1940 a pair of Gannets arrived on Ortac, a pinnacle of rock between Burhou and the Casquets. A few weeks later the entire population of Alderney was evacuated ahead of the invading German forces. By the time they returned, five years later, several

Reefs and Islets

hundred pairs of Gannets were breeding on Ortac and on the pinnacles closer to the coast called the Garden Rocks. Numbers have steadily increased and now an astounding five thousand pairs breed here every year. Ocean wanderers, Gannets only come ashore to breed with the earliest birds returning in February. The males arrive first to claim a nest site announcing their ownership with loud calls and a bowing display with wings held outstretched. Space in the colony is at a premium and, armed with such long, sharp beaks, fights can be fierce and frequent. Once the nest site is established the male signals for a mate by shaking his head rapidly from side to side. The pair build the nest together, a substantial platform of seaweed and other flotsam collected at sea. The ingredients of the Gannet's nest are a sad reflection on the state of our seas for much of it is nylon fishing net, rope and plastics that the birds find drifting on the surface. Such resilient fibres can prove fatal to the growing chick, should it get tangled. The adults are unconcerned by the source of their nesting material and will often steal pieces of an unguarded neighbouring nest to add to their own. Throughout this period of construction the courtship ritual continues with noisy greetings and a gentle jousting with their beaks called 'bill fencing'.

The largest bird in the north Atlantic, the Gannet Morus bassanus *comes ashore only to breed. They choose to nest closely together yet often squabble violently with their neighbours and readily steal each other's nesting material. As numbers continue to increase it will be interesting to see if they colonise any other rock stacks in the Channel Islands.*

Wildlife of the Channel Islands

The Gannet's single white egg is laid from mid-April onwards and, lacking a brood patch, the parents use their large webbed feet to keep the egg warm. Six weeks later the chick hatches and the constant burbling cackle of the colony gradually rises to an incessant roar as their numbers are swollen still further. The weather is now at its hottest and both adults and parents flap their throats in an effort to keep cool. Crammed together, the birds ferociously protect their offspring and will not hesitate in delivering a nasty stab wound if a neighbour wanders too close. Any sudden movement can provoke an attack so before flying they signal their intent by pointing upwards before taking to the sky. Unable to fly, the youngsters have their own form of protection. As they mature their fluffy down is replaced by black plumage which is thought to help them avoid being mistaken for a trespassing adult. Thirteen weeks after hatching they lurch off the cliffs in a clumsy glide and belly-flop into the sea. Too heavy to take off again they must wait a week or so until their excess fat reserves are used up and they can begin their life on the wing. While travelling Gannets skim low over the waves but are at their most impressive when hunting. They feed on fish, particularly mackerel, and circle high above the sea in search of their prey. Once spotted they fold their wings back and plunge headfirst into the water, reaching speeds of around sixty miles per hour (100kph) as they hit the surface. Excellent eyesight, a lack of external nostrils and a toughened skull enable them to feed in such a spectacular manner.

The distinctive colouring on the beak of the Puffin Fratercula arctica *is merely an outer layer developed for the breeding season then shed in the winter to reveal a smaller, duller bill. The dark ornamentation around the eye fades and its plumage is generally more subdued in the colder months which it spends far out at sea (SoA).*

A gangly youth not yet able to fly but once fully grown the Great Black-backed Gull Larus marinus *will dwarf all of the other species of gull. Powerful and opportunist, it will take smaller birds, and their eggs and chicks, and may partly be responsible for the local decrease in Puffins numbers.*

Two miles north-west of Alderney lies the islet of Burhou, separated from the main island by the Swinge, a stretch of water infamous for its strong currents, swirling overfalls and scattering of half tide rocks. Low-lying at no more than 25 metres above sea level, Burhou is home to the largest breeding colony of Puffins in the English Channel, although small numbers do breed on Jersey, Herm and near Sark. The gently sloping grassy banks are honeycombed with burrows, some excavated by the birds themselves, others commandeered from the resident Rabbit population. The birds begin returning to land in mid-March and prepare the burrow and nest chamber before getting down to the noisy bill-tapping and head-bobbing that makes up their courtship dance. In early May the single egg is laid and it hatches about six weeks later. The chick, or Puffling, remains in the darkness of its burrow for the first few weeks of its life, fed by its parents early in the morning and late in the afternoon. After a month it reaches its maximum weight and adult feathers form beneath the brown fluffy down. Restless now, the Puffling wanders up and down the burrow exercising its legs and wings. Parental attention diminishes and two weeks later the down is shed in a sudden moult to reveal the glossy black plumage of a young adult. On a warm July evening, driven by hunger, it ventures to the mouth of the burrow and, under cover of darkness, tumbles and flutters into the sea; from the warm, dark security of the burrow to the cold, wet world of the ocean in a matter of moments. Instinct urges it away from the dangers of the shore and by dawn it will be several miles out to sea and, with luck, safe from the predatory gulls. With its short wings, top-heavy bill and large feet, the Puffin looks clumsy in the air and on land but underwater it is transformed into a graceful hunter. Feeding on small fishes, mostly Sand Eel, it needs every bit of its speed and agility. Capable of diving to ten metres and staying underwater for over a minute, it uses its wings for propulsion and its feet as rudders. Sadly the numbers of this charismatic seabird are in steep decline. In the past they were so plentiful that, in the nineteenth century, Guernsey fishermen used to collect their eggs, a practice called 'barbeloting' after the Guernsey French name for the Puffin *barbelote*. (During the Second World War gull and tern eggs were also collected when islanders and occupying forces alike faced extreme food shortages.) In 1949 many of Burhou's Puffins perished during an infestation of blood-sucking mites thought to have been bought accidentally to the island from a nearby chicken farm. However, the colony recovered and reports from the 1960s tell of thousands of pairs breeding on Burhou and several hundred at other sites in the Islands. The smaller colonies are now reduced to a few dozen at most and there are thought to be less than two hundred pairs on Burhou. Whether such a dramatic decrease is due to oil pollution far out at sea where they spend the winter or the factory style fishing for Sand Eel, their staple food, is uncertain. On Burhou the increasing numbers of gulls breeding on the island are certainly taking their toll. They mob the adults carrying food to their chicks and steal their catch and the larger Black-back Gulls will even snatch and kill an adult Puffin in flight. Internationally, Puffin numbers are high with millions living off northern Britain and inside the Arctic circle but these comical looking seabirds would be sorely missed if they ceased breeding in the Channel Islands.

Tiny and bat-like, the best chance of seeing a Storm Petrel Hydrobates pelagicus *is far out at sea where they often follow ships, fluttering back and forth across the wake (MD).*

Reefs and Islets

There is another even more elusive seabird breeding on Burhou and, although its population too is in decline, it is still thought to number about one hundred and fifty pairs. The Storm Petrel is Europe's smallest seabird reaching little more than the size of a sparrow when fully grown. Yet it spends most of its life in the stormy seas of the Atlantic Ocean and returns to land only to breed. Like all petrels, it is named after St Peter from its habit of apparently walking on water. They seldom alight preferring instead to flutter above the sea and patter their tiny webbed feet on the surface while dipping their beak in search of plankton, fish oil and offal. They nest entirely out of sight in burrows or holes between rocks, returning under cover of the darkest nights. Often the only indication of their presence is the soft, purring noise they make while brooding. The single egg is laid in June and is relatively large, representing about a quarter of the female's body weight. Imagine a human mother giving birth to a baby proportionally so immense. Within days the chick develops a thick down and can maintain its own body temperature, freeing both parents to spend the daylight hours far out at sea collecting food. Initially the chick is fed an oily mixture of pre-digested food and in little more than a month is as heavy as its parents. By the time it fledges a couple of weeks later its plumage is glossy and thick unlike that of the adult Storm Petrels which by now is faded and worn, clearly showing the effects of weeks of parental labour. Their breeding finished for the year, the parents join the juveniles as they head away from land and begin their migration southward at the end of the summer.

A fully qualified local? This youngster is one of a group of Atlantic Grey Seals Halichoerus grypus *often seen on a reef off Alderney but whether or not they breed in the Islands is uncertain. Born in early autumn, the pup would have fed on its mother's incredibly rich milk for just three weeks before being abandoned and left to fend for itself.*

The off-shore reefs of Alderney are also home to another, less secretive, form of wildlife; the Atlantic Grey Seal. While lone individuals are seen occasionally all around the Islands, with one or two apparently resident on Les Écréhous and Les Minquiers reefs, the Alderney seals are the only group large enough to be described as a colony. Why there are so few around the islands is something of a mystery. The extensive reefs harbour plenty of prey and there is no shortage of rocks to haul out on. Large numbers thrive to the south-west in Brittany and north on the coasts of Devon and Cornwall yet the group in Alderney number only around twenty. There are adults of both sexes and some juveniles which may indicate that they breed in the Islands. Fully grown, the male is a formidable creature well over two metres long with a distinctive 'roman' nose. The female is smaller, more slightly built and barely half his weight. Masters of the underwater world, they are graceful and incredibly agile travelling at impressive speeds to catch their prey of fish and crustaceans. Each seal needs around 5 kilos (11lb) of food a day so local fishermen ought to be grateful that there are so few in the Channel Islands.

The sheer variety of birds that breed on L'Étac near Sark make it one of the best sites for seabird watching in the Channel Islands. An hour spent bobbing nearby in a boat on an early summer day may be rewarded with sightings of all eight or nine species that breed here.

The island of Sark also has its fair share of reefs and islets, indeed its coastal waters are particularly well endowed with granite outcrops and half-tide rocks, the smaller ones known locally as *boues*. There are two main bird colonies, one on the stacks off the west coast called Les Autelets and the other, to the south, called L'Étac.

The local population boom of the Fulmar Fulmarus glacialis is even more impressive considering the fact that they take nine or ten years to mature and rear only one chick a year. They are incredibly long-lived with some reaching over forty years old (MD).

Ungainly on land, Razorbills Alca torda *are at their most adept underwater. Similar in appearance to the more plentiful Guillemots, they can be distinguished by their flattened beak with obvious white stripe.*

The latter is an almost triangular pinnacle rising some sixty metres above sea level and home to an impressive variety of seabirds. Puffins breed in burrows on the lower grassy slopes and Oystercatchers rear their chicks on rocky outcrops surprisingly close to the sea. Razorbills, Guillemots and Shags nest on the ledges higher up while Fulmars and Herring Gulls tend to nest even further up the cliffs. The very highest point, as is often the way, is ruled by the Great Black-backed Gulls. The Fulmar is perhaps the most easily overlooked appearing, superficially, very much like a small gull. The tubular nostrils on its beak, however, reveal that it actually belongs to a different order, the *Procellariiformes* or tubenoses, and is related to the Albatross and Petrel. Relative newcomers to the Channel Islands, Fulmars were originally a northern species most often associated with the waters of the Arctic. At the end of the nineteenth century they began extending their range to the south, for reasons still unknown, and bred here for the first time in the 1970s. Superb fliers, they can skim the undulating swell with effortless grace or ride the turbulent air currents of a windswept cliff with ease. Faithful to both their nest site and their mate, the Fulmars' courtship ritual is a noisy, cackling affair of head-waving and bowing with the beak wide open to reveal the striking mauve colour inside. The single, white egg takes over fifty days to hatch and it is a further two months before the fledgling can fly. If disturbed both parents and chicks can eject from their mouth a foul-smelling oily liquid aimed with some force and accuracy at the unfortunate intruder. But this form of deterrent relies on more than just its pungent odour as a well documented incident on the south coast of England revealed. A female Peregrine Falcon was continuously attacked by a pair of Fulmars as she brooded her eggs in a hollow near their nest. Eventually the Falcon's beautiful plumage was so badly caked that she could not hunt and she would have died of starvation had she not been rescued, cleaned and nursed back to health.

The rock pinnacles of Les Autelets on the west coast of Sark are home to the largest breeding colony of Guillemots in the Channel Islands

Reefs and Islets

Like many seabirds, Guillemots Uria aalge *come ashore only to breed and spend the rest of their life at sea.*

In contrast to L'Étac, the rock stacks of Les Autelets are home to just one species of seabird: the Guillemot. In summer the narrow ledges are crammed with birds and the nearby cliffs resound to their constant guttural *aaargh* call. In Guernsey French they are called *âne de maire* a reference possibly to their call sounding something like a donkey's bray. In both appearance and behaviour they are very similar to the Razorbill but the latter can easily be distinguished by its flattened, square-ended beak as compared to the Guillemot's round bill. Both look for all the world like tiny penguins and breed in quarrelsome colonies crammed tightly together. No nest as such is constructed by the Guillemot, instead the parents lay their single egg directly on to the rock, trusting that its pear shape will prevent it from rolling off the ledge and into the sea. The chick hatches after just thirty days and develops rapidly until, only eighteen days later, it half flutters and half tumbles into the water. Its father flies down to join it and calls to the youngster drawing it further out to sea where it is less likely to be picked off by the scavenging gulls. Groups of these flightless juveniles paddle together to form nursery rafts where the parents continue to feed their offspring while encouraging them to dive for their own food. Like Puffins they are superbly adapted to life underwater. Occassionally a lucky scuba diver is treated to a virtuoso performance of breathtaking speed and agility as a group flash past streaming a trail of tiny silver bubbles. Strong swimmers, Guillemots are propelled by their feet as well as their wings and are able to dive over fifty metres deep. Not until some three weeks later do the juveniles fly yet it makes perfect sense that birds which spend most of their time at sea learn to swim before taking to the air.

Left: Bréhon Tower was built in 1855 and lies at the southern end of the Little Russel, the tide-swept channel between Guernsey and Herm.

Below: The male Common Tern Sterna hirundo *impresses his mate with an elaborate display both on the ground and in the air. His posturing is made all the more appealing by the constant supply of small fish he presents as part of his courtship dance (MD).*

Reefs and Islets

Almost directly west of Sark's Guillemot colony a round stone tower squats in the swirling channel between Guernsey and Herm. This is Bréhon Tower, a Victorian fortress built, like so many others, to protect the Islands from a French invasion that never came. Long since deserted, the tower is silent for much of the year but in summer its ramparts ring to the harsh cries of the 'swallow of the sea', the Common Tern. Returning from their winter retreat off the equatorial coast of west Africa in April, Terns breed on several remote reefs and fortifications around the Islands. Courtship is an elaborate affair with a great deal of aerial displaying and ground-based posturing during which the male presents his intended with a continuous supply of fish. Their breeding is synchronised, with every pair in the colony laying its clutch of two or three eggs within a week of each other. As soon as all the eggs have hatched the meagre nest is abandoned and the chicks hide close by while the adults go in search of food. With their forked tail and graceful, fluttering flight they are impossible to confuse with the larger gulls and are at their most elegant while feeding. They hover above their prey of small fish and make delicate headlong dives just below the surface of the sea. But their fragile appearance disguises a pugnacious character revealed only too well to those who threaten the colony. Intruders are dive-bombed and screamed at in anger and the diminutive Tern will have no hesitation in striking even a human interloper should they venture too close to its chick.

Part of the Jersey parish of St Martin, Les Écréhous are popular with visiting boats from Jersey and France. Most of the summer houses are on the smaller island, La Marmotière, while Le Maître Île (in the background) is left mostly to the seabirds.

Wildlife of the Channel Islands

The remains of a hut and a thirteenth century priory on Le Maître Île are now the domain of the gulls and Shags that breed there. The prominent raised nests in front of the ruins belong to the Cormorants.

The north coast of Jersey hardly needs any man-made fortifications to repel human invaders for its sheer cliffs are almost completely guarded by offshore stacks and reefs. The Pierres de Lecq, more often simply called the Paternosters, rise jagged and sheer two miles off the north-west corner and further east are the lower lying Dirouilles. Both are wave-swept in the stormiest weather with little or no permanent vegetation. Further east again lies a larger reef system, Les Écréhous. Exactly half way between Jersey and the coast of Normandy, its ownership has been the subject of much contention over the years. As late as 1956 the French disputed Jersey's claim to the reef taking their case to the International Court of Justice at The Hague. Jersey's sovereignty was upheld but challenged again in 1994 when a flotilla of French fishermen from the nearby port of Carteret landed on the reef. A force of Jersey policemen were dispatched to keep order and protect the island's flag but the 'invasion' was a symbolic one, more to do with fishing rights than real estate. In the previous century a Jersey fisherman, Phillipe Pinel, lived on the reef for forty-six years declaring himself King of Les Écréhous. When Queen Victoria visited Jersey in 1857 he presented to her a basket he had woven of dried seaweed. In more recent times another Jerseyman lived on the reef and he too declared himself sovereign. Alphonse Le Gastelois 'emigrated' to Les Écréhous in 1961 after being wrongly suspected of a series of terrifying assaults on children, and lived there alone for fourteen years.

The chicks and eggs of the Herring Gull Larus argentatus *are vulnerable to attack by their own kind if left unattended. If they can survive these dangerous early days the chicks will take a further four years to reach maturity and gain the grey and gleaming white plumage of an adult.*

Les Écréhous consists of two main islands, Le Maître Île and La Marmotière, along with an impressive shingle bank and countless outlying rocks and sandbanks. The vegetation struggles to grow in the shallow soil and was further reduced on Le Maître Île by the constant grazing of Rabbits which were introduced early in the twentieth century. They eventually disappeared but were reintroduced in the 1970s. Just five years later they had eaten every scrap of foliage on the larger island except a pungent plant called Stinking Iris which they would not touch even though they were starving. As soon as the Rabbits were removed the vegetation recovered and almost seventy species of plant have been recorded as surviving in the salt-laden atmosphere of the reef. It is an important breeding site for hundreds of seabirds with Common Terns, Gulls, Shags, and Cormorants all adding their voices to the springtime hubbub. Some are easily disturbed by the increasing numbers of human visitors to Les Écréhous but the most resilient and numerous, as elsewhere in the Islands, are the Herring Gulls. With their gleaming white plumage and evocative wailing call, to some this most common of gull is the very essence of the seaside. Without doubt they provide a magnificent sight effortlessly riding the currents of a wind-swept cliff or following the wake of a fishing boat at sea. However Herring Gulls are opportunists and able to eat almost anything. Some have forsaken their traditional coastal nesting sites and moved into residential areas. Just as comfortable on a chimney pot as a cliff face, their early morning calls and inability to resist raiding unprotected rubbish bags have not endeared them to their human neighbours. Some have become so bold as to take food unbidden almost literally from our mouths and many a small child has had an ice cream snatched from its hand in a dare-devil aerial swoop. Signs at the Islands' beach cafés and outdoor restaurants advise against feeding the birds and covered bins have been designed to curtail their refuse raids. But much rubbish is still left unattended and the gulls remain one step ahead. Their numbers in urban areas continue to increase but maybe we only have ourselves to blame?

Stretching for over eight miles from east to west, Les Minquiers reef is wisely given a wide berth by commercial shipping.

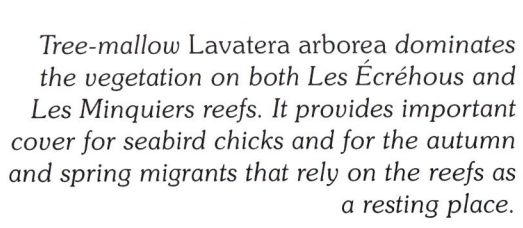

Tree-mallow Lavatera arborea *dominates the vegetation on both Les Écréhous and Les Minquiers reefs. It provides important cover for seabird chicks and for the autumn and spring migrants that rely on the reefs as a resting place.*

Reefs and Islets

The most southerly point of the Channel Islands, and therefore of the British Isles, is Les Minquiers, an extensive reef lying halfway between Jersey and St Malo. Like Les Écréhous, its ownership has been the subject of much disagreement with the French government and for many years Jersey had to man a customs post on both reefs. On the highest tide little more than a tenth of a hectare of the main island, Maîtresse Île, is left above sea level. Low water reveals a very different scene when almost forty square miles (100 sq km) of rock, sand bank and shallow lagoon are uncovered. With such a small area for plants to grow in, it is not surprising that fewer than twenty species have been recorded on the reef. That any of these have survived at all is something of a miracle when, in the autumn and winter of 1972/73, weedkiller was sprayed over virtually all of the vegetation. This extraordinary act was part of an ill-conceived plan to cover the island in non-native conifers, supposedly in the name of conservation. The reef belongs ultimately to the Crown and an appeal was made to Her Majesty's Receiver-General which successfully prevented the trees being planted. However, the damage was already done. The vegetation there was of the kind perfectly adapted to withstand the rigors of winter storms, salt spray and summer drought and it was wiped out in one stroke. With it went the ground cover and associated insects so vital to migrating birds in spring and autumn. Erosion followed where much of the precious soil was left bare. Over the next few years the vegetation slowly returned and now Sea Beet and Tree-mallow are again abundant but some of the original plant species are yet to return.

With its oily-green plumage, yellow gape and comical crest, the Shag Phalacrocorax aristotelis *in spring plumage is a handsome bird.*

Rows of Shags drying their wings and warming up after a fishing expedition are a familiar sight on rocks and reefs all around the Channel Islands.

The most common breeding bird on Les Minquiers is the Shag, a diving bird often mistaken for the larger Cormorant. To confuse things even more both species breed on the reef although the Cormorant is far less numerous. Both are expert fishermen, relying on sand eel and small fish, and they often jump clear of the water when they dive. In order to be less buoyant underwater, and therefore able to swim with more ease, they have sacrificed the water-repelling plumage of other seabirds. The downside to this is that they literally get soaked to the skin, and presumably very cold, and so must stand in the familiar heraldic posture with wings outstretched to dry their feathers after a bout of fishing. Shags breed early in the season because their chicks take a long time to fledge, over fifty days, and are dependent on their parents for another month after that. When they first hatch the chicks are blind and bald with a distinctly reptilian appearance. The nest is an untidy heap of vegetation on a sheltered ledge or among boulders made highly visible by liberal streaks of white guano. Common all around the Islands, perhaps the best place to see a Shag in its real element, underwater, is in one of the harbours where lone birds often hunt beneath the fishing boats, cruisers and yachts.

A view of Les Amfroques from the north coast of Herm. Known locally as 'The Humps' this cluster of six tiny islets is a valuable breeding site for the Cormorant, Shag, Guillemot, Razorbill and Puffin as well as three species of gull.

Wildlife of the Channel Islands

There remains one final bird to mention in an account of the wildlife on the offshore reefs and islets although it might easily be included in the chapter on cliffs. The Oystercatcher is the Island's most numerous breeding wader. With its distinctive black and white plumage and dark orange eyes and beak, it is impossible to mistake for any other bird. It has an eclectic appetite and will probe the sand for worms and cockles or use its powerful beak to hammer shellfish off the rocks. In winter local Oystercatchers are joined by many others from further north and, as the rising tide pushes them off their feeding grounds, hundreds gather together to roost. Crowded just a beak's length apart they often share their roost with Curlews, Turnstones, Plovers and Sanderling although each species stays very much with its own kind. The Oystercatcher's nest is a simple scrape in the turf just above the rocks or amongst pebbles on the beach. In common with many seabirds, the chicks are mottled and well disguised and leave the nest as soon as they can walk. Should an intruder threaten their offspring the parents let out a shrill piping call, one of the quintessential sounds of the cliffs, reefs and islets of the Channel Islands.

One of the few waders to breed in the Islands in any number, the Oystercatcher Haematopus ostalegus *is impossible to confuse with any other species. Here a pair roost at high water with their newly-fledged offspring.*

A juvenile cormorant Phalacrocorax Carbo *digesting its seafood meal on the north coast of Jersey.*

The shimmering shingle of Herm's Shell Beach is made up entirely of seashells and their broken fragments dredged up from the deep by tide and storm. Wild Leek Allium ampeloprasum, *in the foreground, is one of the many wildflowers to thrive on the island's cliff tops.*

Chapter Three

Beaches and Dunes

The essential ingredient of any seaside holiday is sand. Warm dry sand to lie on while snoozing in the sun and damp sand just the right consistency for building castles. Yet the stuff we love to feel between our toes and mould with bucket and spade forms the foundation of a whole ecosystem. Many plants and animals have evolved to thrive on the beach and the dunes as well as the maritime heath beyond the tide's reach.

The shores of the Channel Islands are blessed with a wonderful variety of beaches. Some form secretive sandy coves between sheer granite cliffs and are revealed only when the tide retreats. Sark only has these 'part time' beaches but the strenuous walk down, and more importantly the hike back up again, is amply rewarded by the view from sea level. Jersey's east and south coasts have broad sandy bays and almost the whole of the west coast is taken up by the magnificent storm beach of St Ouen's Bay. In Guernsey and Alderney the widest stretches of sand sweep along the northern half of the islands. On low water many more miles of golden sand bar and shingle bank are exposed offshore around the numerous reefs and islets. Strong tides surge through the narrow channels between the islands and scour the seabed of its natural treasures. Off the northern end of Herm these currents swirl into shallow water laden with millions of seashells creating the best known stretch of seashore in the Channel Islands, Shell Beach. Half a mile long and made entirely of seashells and their broken fragments, Shell Beach is unique in its formation within the British Isles. The huge variety of species has attracted shell collectors since Victorian times and, even today, few visitors who stroll along the gleaming white shingle are unable to resist the tiny works of art at their feet.

Each shell is a marvel of natural engineering which survives long after the creature that formed it has gone. Few live long enough to die of old age but fall victim to other marine life or are even eaten by their own kind. Others perish when they are washed up on the shore and pecked from their shells by predatory birds. Each shell is a calcareous structure laid down by the mantle, a delicate tissue that cloaks the soft main body of the animal. The shape, colour and texture of the shell reflects the lifestyle and environment it lived in. The Razor shell, for example, is long, smooth and slender allowing it to slip easily and quickly beneath the sand. Limpets form a sturdy, broad-based cone which dissipates the force of the waves that pound the rocks on which they cling. Many of the gastropods,

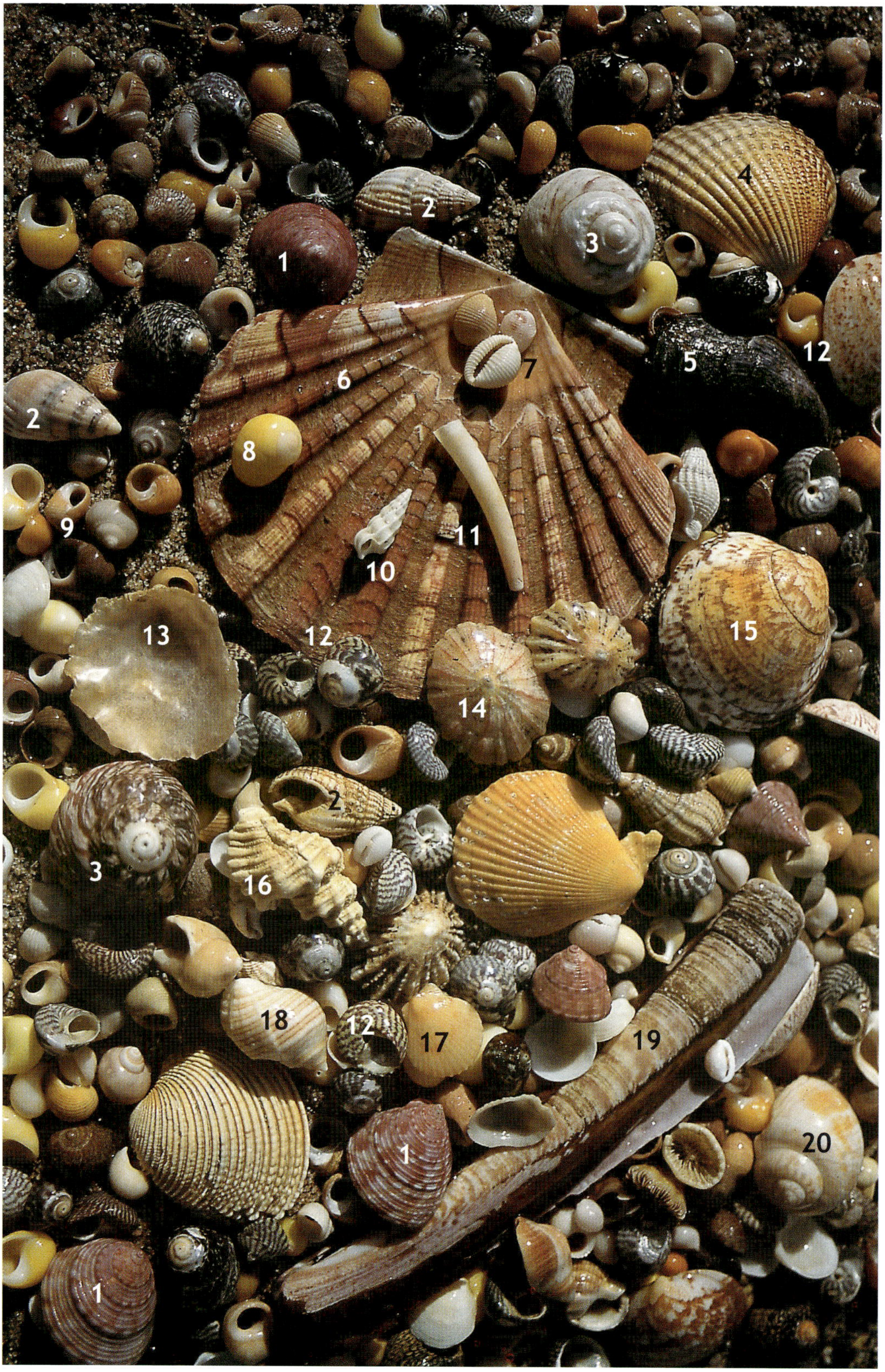
1
2
3
4
2
6
7
5
12
8
9
11
10
13
12
15
14
2
3
16
18
12
17
19
1
20
1

Beaches and Dunes

Opposite: Just a few of the hundred or so species of seashell found in the waters around the Channel Islands.

1. Painted Topshell *Calliostoma zizyphinum*
2. Netted Dog-whelk *Hinia reticulata*
3. Turban Topshell *Gibbula magus*
4. Common Cockle *Cerastoderma edule*
5. Common Mussel *Mytilus edulis*
6. Great Scallop *Pecten maximus*
7. Cowrie *Trivia monacha*
8. Flat Periwinkle *Littorina obtusata*
9. Common Periwinkle *Littorina littorea*
10. Common Wentletrap *Epitonium clathrus*
11. Tusk Shell *Dentalium vulgare*
12. Purple Topshell *Gibbula umbilicalis*
13. Saddle Oyster *Anomia ephippium*
14. Limpets *Patella* sp
15. Dog Cockle *Glycymeris glycymeris*
16. Oyster Drill *Ocenebra erinacea*
17. Queen Scallop *Aequipecten opercularis*
18. Dog Whelk *Nucella lapillus*
19. Common Razor Shell *Ensis ensis*
20. Necklace Shell *Polinices polianus*

---

spiral-shaped shells, also thrive in the turbulent realm where sea meets land. They too fasten tightly to the rocks and most congregate in the shade while the tide is out. They have also developed an extra line of defence in the form of a tiny trap door, called an operculum. This perfectly fits the opening of the shell, firmly sealing the entrance to keep moisture in and hunters out. Pluck any type of winkle off a rock and the closing 'lid' is clearly visible. Shells made of two halves, bivalves, often live below the seabed. Many, like the Cockle, have thick shells with ridges and corrugations to give them added strength and protection against the probing beaks of seabirds.

Eventually all seashells succumb to the lashing of the waves and their fragments blend with ground-down particles of rock to form sand. Beneath the waves its shifting mass is piled in great rippled banks that constantly move with the tide. Seaweeds find it impossible to colonise such a mobile environment but in areas sheltered from the worst of the tidal currents, lush green meadows carpet the seabed. This is Eel Grass, not a seaweed but a flowering plant, the only one of its kind in the British Isles to have adapted to life in the sea. Its long, slender leaves grow from rhizomes beneath the sand and, in summer, spikes of flowers appear near the base. Male and female flowers grow next to each other and, with no need to attract insects to pollinate them, are dull and inconspicuous relying entirely on the tide to spread their cloud of pollen. In the 1930s great swathes of Eel Grass were wiped out by a mystery disease and the plant's need for sheltered, shallow waters means it often suffers when land is reclaimed from the sea. It is unclear exactly how these losses affect the marine environment as a whole but it is well known that Eel Grass beds provide a nursery ground for many different fish including some commercially important species. Hordes of other creatures make their homes among the leaves or burrow in the soft sediment between the stems. Eel Grass is also the favourite food of one of the Islands' most popular winter visitors, the Brent Geese.

Right: Eel Grass Zostera marina *is a haven for all sorts of marine life. The shorter species* Zostera nana, *which survives further up the shore, is vital to the Brent Geese that overwinter in the Channel Islands.*

Below: A family group of Brent Geese Branta bernicla. *Guided by their parents, the youngsters have flown over a thousand miles from their Arctic birthplace (MD).*

Beaches and Dunes

In the middle of September the first Brent Geese touch down in the Channel Islands having flown over a thousand miles from their breeding grounds in the Arctic. This journey is even more remarkable considering the stature of this long-distance traveller, for the Brent is barely larger than a Mallard Duck. The Islands play host to two distinct races. Those with dark bellies breed in Russia, while smaller numbers with pale bellies fly in from the high Canadian Arctic. Both feed upended in shallow water with their tails pointing skywards revealing bright white underparts as they graze. If Eel Grass is in short supply the geese will eat sea lettuce and other green seaweeds and at high tide move inland to graze in fields. Shy and difficult to approach, Brent Geese constantly call to each other with a quiet, nasal vronk-vronk, one of the most haunting sounds of the winter. When they leave in April for their northern breeding grounds the seashores of the Channel Islands seem an emptier place.

Much sought after by birds, fish and fishermen, the Lugworm Arenicola marina *moves close to the surface every forty five minutes or so to eject the sand it has passed through its body, forming the familiar worm casts.*

These green puddles are masses of tiny Mint Sauce Worms Convoluta roscoffensis, *a species unique to Channel Islands and nearby French coast. Sensitive to vibration, walking near a patch causes them to dissolve into the sand in seconds (RL).*

Wildlife of the Channel Islands

Great stretches of sand and sediment uncovered as the tide retreats appear barren at any time of year, yet beneath the surface live a mass of small creatures. Shellfish, shrimps and segmented worms make up the majority of this fauna, some so tiny that they live in the spaces between grains of sand. The larger invertebrates are more obvious, leaving clues to their lifestyles in the holes and patterns they create on the surface. Others are more obscure such as the minuscule Mint Sauce Worms, which congregate on the surface in their thousand but are still so easy to overlook. Less than half a centimetre long, each of these flattened, oval worms has microscopic algae living within its body, hence their bright green colour. When the tide goes out the worms wriggle to the surface en masse allowing the chlorophyll in their algae to photosynthesise, that is, produce sugars from sunlight. Once nourished the solar-powered worms sink back into the sand before they are washed away by the returning tide. Experiments have shown that even when taken many miles from their home the extraordinary worms continue to rise and fall in the sand in exact rhythm with the tides of the Islands. Like all of the burrowers and sand dwellers they are vital, protein-packed components in the food chain that supports much of the marine and bird life on the seashore.

Hundreds of Dunlin Calidris alpina spend the winter in the Islands, their numbers swollen by those passing through on their way to feeding grounds further south (MD).

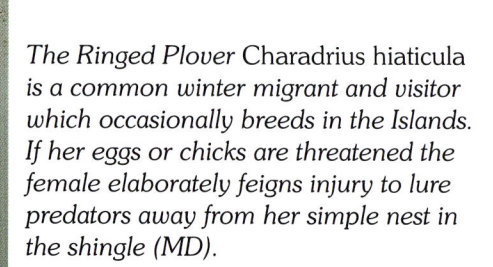

The Ringed Plover Charadrius hiaticula is a common winter migrant and visitor which occasionally breeds in the Islands. If her eggs or chicks are threatened the female elaborately feigns injury to lure predators away from her simple nest in the shingle (MD).

Beaches and Dunes

For those with a passion for bird life, the winter is without doubt the best time to visit the coast. As the days draw in and the first of the autumn gales gather strength some of the thousands of waders that overwinter in the Channel Islands have already alighted. As the trees lose their leaves the numbers increase and the wintry weather further north drives more birds to the relatively mild climate of the Islands. At high tide the roosts are packed with birds all angled like weather vanes into the wind and crammed within a beak's length of each other. Each species crowds with others of its kind with the larger birds, such as Curlews, Oystercatchers and Egrets, dominating the highest part of the rocks. The smaller waders have to make do with ledges closer to the water.

As the tide begins to fall and the seashore uncovers, the birds leave their roosts to feed. Many depart, as they arrived, in swirling streams of tightly packed flocks which pour from the rocks in a breathtaking display of aerobatics. Dunlin are particularly accomplished close formation fliers. They form fluid, tapering lines which seem to disappear in an instant as the birds simultaneously bank hiding their grey upper parts and revealing much paler undersides. As the flock twists the other way the birds shimmer back into view before tumbling out of the air to land near the water's edge. Feeding begins on touch-down with heads lowered and beaks frantically probing the sand. Often quarrelsome and noisy, they run along the shore with a harsh treeep call. They are sometimes joined by groups of Sanderling, similar in size but much paler than the Dunlin. Sanderling also feed in a frenzy of activity at the sea's edge, darting forward to pick off the tiny shrimps revealed by each wave before running back out of the water's reach.

With so many hungry birds searching for food competition is great but evolution has ensured that each species is equipped to hunt a slightly different prey. The Curlew is the largest of the Islands' waders and also has the longest beak. Slender and curving downwards, it has a sensitive tip that can detect worms, shellfish and crabs deep under the sand. Oystercatchers also feed in the sand but their shorter, stronger beaks are also used to hammer shellfish off rocks and smash them open. The smaller waders have bills of differing length and shape which allow them to feed at various depths in the sand and so live together without competing for the same food. Turnstones have yet another approach to the feeding game. They have short chisel-shaped beaks and powerful neck muscles and, as their name suggests, they flip over small stones snapping up the tiny invertebrates they uncover. They are also capable of 'bulldozing' quite sizeable piles of seaweed in search of a meal. Small and streaked red-brown, they are not always easy to see and it is often only the chinking sound of pebbles being moved that gives away their presence. Add to this the piping squeaks and chatter of other small waders, the melodic burble of the Curlew and the echoing shriek of the Oystercatcher and you have a perfect soundscape of the seashore in winter.

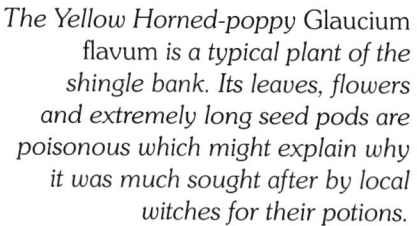

The Yellow Horned-poppy Glaucium flavum *is a typical plant of the shingle bank. Its leaves, flowers and extremely long seed pods are poisonous which might explain why it was much sought after by local witches for their potions.*

By spring many of the waders have left for their northern breeding grounds but, as if to compensate for their absence, the lengthening days and rising temperatures generate an abundance of wildflowers. None can survive the twice daily drenching of the beach itself but, incredibly, some have evolved to thrive in the shingle just above the high tide line. This is a harsh place in which to live. The plants here are lashed by salt spray and the friction of stones rubbing together inhibits their growth. Yet the same grinding motion ensures a constant supply of lime as shells cast up on the shore are broken down. The shingle itself preserves the fresh water beneath it which, being lighter, floats on the denser salt water. Rotting vegetation blown up the beach gets trapped between the pebbles creating a toe-hold for any seeds that land there. Sea Kale is typical of these so-called 'pioneering' plants with its long, thin tap root and sumptuous mounds of thick, leathery leaves. An edible plant, it is said to taste like asparagus but its leaves are tough and unappetising. Samphire, on the other hand, has been considered a delicacy for centuries and was collected in all of the Islands. The fleshy stems were lightly simmered and eaten as a vegetable while the leaves were boiled in vinegar to make a strong pickle. So highly prized was this plant in the seventeenth century that a Sark man was arrested for stealing it from the cliffs of neighbouring Brecqhou. Samphire still thrives in the Islands but, despite its culinary value, is no longer harvested commercially.

Among the stems of these hardy seaside plants live the first of the coastal animals. The most obvious are clusters of small, stripy snails that cram together in the hottest weather on the stalks of Wild Radish and Sea Beet. These are Pisan Snails, originally a Mediterranean species named after the Italian city where they were first identified. Smaller than garden snails and with more distinct bands, quite how these exotic molluscs came to the Islands is unknown. Records show that they were initially found only in Jersey until, in 1860, a Dr Lukis introduced them to Guernsey. By the 1930s they had also spread to Alderney. Like

Above: Edible, but not very appetising, the leathery leaves of Sea Kale Crambe maritima *can retain moisture in the desiccating salt air where it thrives. In summer its grey-green leaves are almost eclipsed by a froth of white flowers.*

Left: The common name for Rock Samphire Crithmum maritimum *is derived from its old name 'herbe Saint-Pierre', a reference to its association with the patron saint of fishermen. Both its old Jersey and Guernsey names contain the name 'Pierre'.*

Left: Pisan Snails Euparypha pisana *are a Mediterranean species which flourish in the salty atmosphere of the seashore even in the hottest weather. Their large numbers attract birds, particularly Song Thrushes.*

Below: The Lesser White-toothed Shrew Crocidura suaveolens, *found in Jersey and Sark, is slightly smaller than the Greater White-toothed Shrew which lives in the other Channel Islands. Both are continental species and so are not found on the British mainland (JED).*

all snails, the Pisans are most active after rain when they slither forth in search of food. Unlike others of their kind, when the weather is hot and dry they do not take cover in the undergrowth but cluster together on the tallest stems. Tightly clamped down to preserve their precious moisture, the combined weight of the snails often visibly weighs down the plants they cling on which they cling.

The boulder-strewn seashore and high tide line also provide a hunting ground for some of the Channel Islands' most interesting small mammals, the White-toothed Shrews. These tiny insectivores live their short lives in bursts of frantic activity followed by similar periods of rest. Their diet of beetles, fly larvae and sandhoppers is low in nourishment so they must eat almost their own body weight each day to survive. Unable to store enough food to hibernate, they forage throughout the winter but live for barely more than a year. Their name refers to the lack of dark red tips to the teeth, one of the distinguishing features that separates them from most other species of shrew. In the Islands there are two different species and their distribution throws up some interesting questions. Jersey and Sark have the Lesser White-toothed Shrew which is the same as that found in France although not until over two hundred miles south and east of the Islands. The Greater White-toothed Shrew of Guernsey also lives in Alderney and Herm as well as throughout France including the coast opposite the Channel Islands. While it makes sense for Jersey to have some different flora and fauna from the rest of the Islands due to its longer connection with the Continent, the fact that it shares a shrew with Sark is something of a mystery. In her book *A Natural History of the Jersey* naturalist Frances Le Sueur puts forward a very plausible theory. When Sark was colonised in the sixteenth century many of the settlers came from St Ouen on the west coast of Jersey. With no real harbour on that side of the island they almost certainly left from a small bay called Grève de Lecq. While stores and materials were piled on the beach before being loaded onto boats it is not impossible that Lesser White-toothed Shrews inadvertently stowed away while searching for food among the pebbles and stones. Once landed in Sark they would then be free to extend their empire. It is only a theory and impossible to prove either way but, as shrews don't fly or swim, they must almost certainly have arrived by boat.

Many of the beaches in the Channel Islands are restrained by a seawall and the land beyond bound by tarmac and buildings. Where the coast has been left to itself the landscape offers us the chance to see every stage in a wonderful biological succession from beach and bare sand to dune and heathland. The very foundation of this environment are the plants that grow directly in the sand, the first rank among the defenders of the shore that secure the land against the inroads of the sea. Like those that grow in the shingle, these plants often have fleshy leaves and thick skin to protect them against the extremes of heat and salinity close to the ocean's edge. Sea Sandwort is typical of these and is so well adapted to this habitat that it grows in bare, salty sand. Its succulent, glossy leaves form dense, low-growing carpets that act as tiny windbreaks causing sand to pile up on its

Sea Sandwort Honkenya peploides *has a strong root system that helps stabilise shifting sands. If buried by a storm or a sudden change in wind direction it sends up new shoots that continue to grow until they reach the surface where they form a new carpet.*

Another seashore specialist Sea Bindweed Calystegia soldanella *has a deep root system to survive the 'mobile' nature of its habitat and to search out fresh water. Its presence in Guernsey has been traced back several thousands of years since its distinctive pollen was found preserved in peat.*

Alderney Sea-lavender Limonium normannicum *is unique to Jersey, Alderney and Normandy and is able to cope not only with salt spray but with complete sea water drenching on spring tides.*

Jersey Thrift Armeria alliacea *is taller and flowers later in the year than the common Thrift and, being less tolerant of salt water, tends to grow slightly further inland.*

leeward side. Sea Bindweed also thrives in these desert-like conditions. Unlike its infamous relative so disliked by gardeners, it does not wrap itself around other plants but instead trails its heart-shaped leaves and pink trumpet flowers over the ground.

Many more lime-loving plants stake their claim in this borderland nourished by the crushed remains of seashells and rotting seaweed blown up from the beach. Sea Holly, Sea Rocket and Sea Spurge compete for space with Hottentot Fig, a rampant garden escape that also smothers great swathes of the Islands' cliffs. More popular among botanists are the Sea-lavenders particularly Alderney Sea-lavender, a species unique to Jersey and Alderney though more common in the larger island. As if not to be outdone, Sark has a variety of Sea-lavender all of its own. Slightly further inshore, sheltered from the worst of the salt spray, grows another Channel Island speciality, Jersey Thrift. Taller than the more common Thrift, it is a native of central and southern Europe, reaching its northern limit in Jersey. It does not grow on the British mainland or in any of the other Channel Islands. It blooms later in the year than the other variety although the flowering times of the two have sometimes overlapped and allowed a hybrid to form.

Les Blanches Banques in St Ouen's Bay in Jersey is one of the most important examples of dune habitat in Europe and home to a rich variety of wildlife including over four hundred species of plants.

Beaches and Dunes

All of these seaside plants help trap and stabilise the sand blown ashore from the beach but the real builders of the dunes are the grasses. Couch Grass lives on the lower slopes, its leaves steadily growing as the sand builds around them. As the slopes gain height the Couch Grass gives way to the longer Marram Grass which also has horizontal rhizomes with long, tough roots that anchor the banks as they grow. Alderney, Herm and Guernsey all have some areas of dune but the largest in the Channel Islands are Les Blanches Banques on the west coast of Jersey. Legend has it that this area was fertile farmland until the fifteenth century. A few islanders had taken to setting false lights on the headland, luring ships to their doom, murdering the crews and pillaging their cargoes. One such victim cursed the land with his dying breath and a year later a terrible storm blew up and sand was blown far inland turning the southern end of St Ouen's bay into an arid wasteland. The invasion of the sand may not have been so sudden but ancient menhirs and piles of pottery found in the dunes show that people lived there as long as five thousand years ago. The whole area must have looked quite different then for the roots and stumps of an ancient coastal forest are sometimes revealed when exceptional storms scour away the sand on the present day shore. The seawall, completed by the occupying German forces in the Second World War, separated the dunes from the beach and cut off their supply of sand. Part of the area was later used as the island's rubbish dump and cars and motorcycles were allowed free access badly eroding the delicate dune system. By the mid 1970s concern among the locals grew so high that the area was eventually protected. Development was strictly regulated and work began to restore much of St Ouen's Bay to its natural state, including years of back-breaking manual labour to replant the valuable Marram. Now the area is recognised as one of the most important dune systems in Europe and it has been declared an SSI, a Site of Special Interest.

Normally cream but sometimes tinged deep pink, the Burnet Rose Rosa pimpinellifolia *spreads rapidly by shooting out suckers and is densely covered in short, sharp spines.*

Fragrant Evening-primrose Oenothera stricta flowers only by night to attract the moths and other night-flying insects that pollinate it. Originally a South American plant, it is another garden escape that fares well in the mild climate of the Islands.

Like the smaller dunes in Alderney, Guernsey and Herm Les Blanches Banques need to be carefully managed for sand dunes are surprisingly fragile. Even the most cautiously placed human feet can damage the surface topsoil and tear the underlying mesh of roots. Once exposed to the elements the drying wind causes the roots to die and the sand around them is swept away causing a 'blow-out', a hole in the dunes that can reach forty metres across. Fencing off vulnerable areas and placing duck-boards as walkways protects the dunes and replanting with Marram helps damaged areas recover. Such care maintains these wonderful wild areas not only for the hundreds of holidaymakers and local people who enjoy them but for the wealth of plants and animals that live there. Most obvious among these are the flowering plants that dapple the dunes with colour and scent the air with their fragrance through the warmer months of the year. Rest-harrow, Medick, Clovers, Bird's-foot Trefoil and numerous species of vetch carpet the ground with their low-growing cushions of flowers. All members of the pea family, they have the ability to transfer nitrogen from the air to the ground, a distinct advantage for any plant growing in poor sandy soil. The Burnet Rose is another ground-hugging plant that flourishes in the dunes. In early summer its creamy white flowers, occasionally tinged with pink, fill the air with their heady, spiced-honey perfume. By autumn the prickly stems are covered with deep purple-black hips, the seed pods that grow from the swollen base of the flowers. Fragrant Evening-primrose, as its name suggests, is another heavily-scented flower. Its perfume is strongest after sunset because this plant is pollinated by moths and other night-flying insects. It shields its flowers by day unfurling them only at dusk. As the morning sun rises next day the yellow flowers droop and darken to orange and by midday they have wilted completely.

The dunes and sandy heathlands beyond them are home to many more flowering plants from the tiny Dwarf Pansy to banks of purple Rough Star-thistle. Some, like Gladiolus and the towering, yellow spikes of Tree Lupin, were originally garden plants which now

Originally bought to the Channel Islands as a garden flower Tree Lupin Lupinus arboreus *now flourishes untended in the sand dunes.*

The Rough Star-thistle Centaurea aspera *grows on the three largest Islands but is most plentiful in the dunes and other sandy areas in Jersey.*

The twisted, tapering lips of the Lizard Orchid's flowers Himantoglossum hircinum *are said to resemble miniature lizards. The second part of its scientific name literally means 'smelling of goat', an accurate description of its perfume (RL).*

The Bee Orchid Ophrys apifera *attracts its pollinators visually and by smell. A real rarity, it is now only known at a couple of locations in Alderney and Guernsey.*

self-seed and flourish in the wild. Others are natives and most precious among them are the orchids. The first to bloom in sandy areas is the Green-winged Orchid, so called because of the five green-veined 'petals' that curve forward to form a hood above the spotted lip of each flower. This is the easiest way of telling it apart from the slightly shorter Early Purple Orchid that also flowers in April and May. Usually rich purple in colour, the Green-winged Orchid occasionally has pink or pure white flowers. It is one of the more common orchids in the Islands but, like all orchids, it is incredibly slow growing and takes several years to develop from a tiny, wind-blown seed.

Once all of the flowers on each spike of the Pyramidal Orchid Anacamptis pyramidalis *are open it loses its characteristic triangular shape. The Hare's-tail Grass* Lagurus ovatus *in the background was once collected and dyed to decorate the floats in Jersey's annual Battle of Flowers which may have aided the plant's spread around the island (RP).*

As spring gives way to summer a much rarer orchid flowers though sadly in very small numbers. The Bee Orchid is one of the Channel Islands' most exotic looking plants. The extraordinary appearance of its flowers has evolved to attract the insects that pollinate them for each of the blooms seem to have a bee at their centre. The flowers take this mimicry a step further by producing a scent that stimulates male bees to attempt sexual union with the bee-shaped petals. During this romantic deception pollen is transferred to the stigma of the plant and its reproductive cycle is triggered. The Lizard Orchid is a much taller plant with flower spikes a metre or more tall. It lacks the bright colours of many other orchids and closer inspection will reveal a rather unpleasant odour of goat. As strange as it is, the Lizard Orchid is also incredibly rare and its single stronghold in Jersey, the only known location in the Channel Islands, is carefully protected. The last orchid to bloom is the Pyramidal, which is much more common and even appears annually on at least one Island golf course. Its spike of deep pink flowers forms a triangular shape as the lowest buds begin to open, hence its name.

Left: Named after the English county where it was first identified, the Essex Skipper Thymelicus lineola *is often seen in company with the bigger Large Skipper. Both species fiercely defend their territories and will chase away bumble-bees and flies as well as other butterflies (RL).*

Below: The Five-spot Burnet Zygaena trifolii *is a day flying moth whose bright colours warn potential predators of its unpalatable taste. Resting on Sea Holly* Eryngium maritimum, *this moth has just emerged from its chrysalis and must dry its wings before taking flight.*

Common Blue butterflies Polyommatus icarus *mating. The female, on the right, has brown wings but the topside of the male's are iridescent blue, a colour not formed by pigments but by the diffraction of sunlight on the thousands of tiny corrugated scales on his wings.*

A pair of Blue-winged Grasshoppers Oedipoda caerulescens *mating. The blue wings that give them their name are revealed only in flight (RL).*

The wealth of flowering plants in the dunes and sandy heathland attracts an equally rich and diverse array of insects. Most obvious among these are the butterflies. While many are easy to follow as they flutter from flower to flower in search of nectar, there are others that move much more quickly. These are skippers and both the Large and Essex species live in the Channel Islands. Unlike most other butterflies, the Skipper's thorax is as long as its wings and it has especially large compound eyes for vision at high speed. At rest it is also easily distinguished by the characteristic attitude in which it holds its wings. The hind-wings are held horizontally and the fore-wings slightly raised, a stance which may help the cold blooded insect absorb vital warmth from the sun.

Butterflies and brightly coloured day-flying moths are the most conspicuous insects but a stroll through the dunes on a warm summer's day will reveal many more miniature natural treasures. The liquid melody of the skylark is accompanied by the vibrating churr of a whole host of crickets and grasshoppers. A good number of these are continental species not found on the British mainland and Jersey even has its own species of grasshopper living nowhere else in the world. Of all these jumping insects the Field Cricket has the loudest and most musical song but visually the most striking is the Blue-winged Grasshopper. As it glides, iridescent blue flashes are revealed on its wings then vanish in an instant as the insect settles. As dusk falls an exotic, throbbing call starts up from the hedges and bramble patches. This belongs to the Great Green Bush-cricket, an enormous insect whose scientific name *Tettigonia viridissima* quite aptly means the greenest of the green.

Of all the insects in the dunes the Ant-lion must be the strangest. The adult can easily be mistaken for a large lacewing or dull-coloured dragonfly but it is the larval stage that is so fascinating. It lives in dry, dusty sand at the centre of a conical pit with its strong jaws just protruding above the surface. The sides of the pit lie at such a critical angle that any small insect that wanders inside triggers a tiny avalanche of sand. As it struggles to escape the larva flicks more sand over its prey until, exhausted, it falls to the centre of the deadly hollow and is dragged below ground by the carnivorous grub.

The profusion of insect life in the dunes and coastal heaths provides the ideal larder for one of the Channel Islands' most spectacular hunters, the Green Lizard. A continental species that failed to reach Britain before the Channel was flooded, the size and vivid colour of this lizard make it impossible to mistake for any other. Like all reptiles it is an ectothermic heliotherm, that is unable to generate its own body heat. Emerging at dawn from a night underground, it is cold and sluggish. Any activity has to be fuelled by basking in the sun or, on a cloudy day, gleaning residual warmth from the rocks. April and May is the breeding season and fierce fights break out among the brightly coloured males as they compete for a mate. In mid-summer the female buries her soft-shelled eggs, up to twenty, in sandy ground warmed by the sun. The young emerge in September, perfect miniatures of their parents and able to fend completely for themselves from the moment they hatch.

Beaches and Dunes

With a little stealth and patience close encounters with the 'dune dragons' are not difficult, especially in the morning when they are still a little cool. What better way to end a stroll on the beautiful beaches and dunes of the Channel Islands.

Left: The Ant-lion Euroleon nostras *spends a year living under ground before it pupates and finally emerges as a winged adult (RL).*

Below: In early summer the male Green Lizard Lacerta bilineata *is at his most splendid and sports a brilliant blue patch on his throat to attract a mate. The female and juveniles are not quite so colourful but often have parallel pale stripes running the length of their backs.*

Seymour Tower stands guard off the south-east coast of Jersey where the tide retreats for almost two miles. If the tide were to fall the same height again the island would be joined to France, as it was during the last ice age.

Chapter Four

Rocky Shores

To fully appreciate the natural history of the Islands' coasts it is vital first to understand the colossal driving force of all life on the seashore; the tide. The Channel Islands experience one of the largest tidal ranges on earth. The waters of the Atlantic sweep through the English Channel and are amplified as they reflect back off the coasts of Brittany and Normandy in the enclosed Bay of St Malo. The Islands lie scattered across the centre of this bay which sees the greatest of these tides in the south. The coast of St Malo itself encounters a difference of up to eighteen metres between high water and low. Jersey has a twelve metre range, Guernsey has ten and Alderney a mere six. These are the most extreme differences measured on spring tides when the gravitational pull of the moon and the sun are strongest on the ocean. 'Spring' tide is a misleading term as these peaks are reached roughly every other week throughout the year whenever there is a full or new moon. It derives from the old English word *springan* which means 'to rise'. The largest of these big tides occurs around the spring and autumn equinox and causes flooding in the Islands if combined with strong enough winds. The periods between the spring tides are called neaps when the sea neither rises so high nor goes out so far. Under these conditions Jersey, for example, has as little as four metres difference between high water and low.

Such enormous quantities of water surging around the Islands create powerful currents and races particularly when squeezed between reefs or forced over shallow shingle banks. Combined with the presence of so many rocks these currents make Channel Island waters treacherous for shipping, a truth sadly illustrated by the wrecks that litter the seabed. For the wildlife the tide is a double-edged sword. It brings with it masses of water-borne food in the form of plankton, the tiny plants and animals that are the basis of all life in the sea. This, along with the Islands' southerly position, has led not only to vast numbers of plants and animals thriving on the seashore but also to a great variety of wildlife, or, to put it more scientifically, a high level of biodiversity.

The disadvantage of such a large tide is that anything living within its range has to survive the twice daily trauma of flood and drought as it flows and ebbs. Imagine then how difficult it must be to live on the seashore. Within six hours water several metres deep creeps away stranding marine animals in shallow pools or leaving them high and dry, exposed to the searing sun and wind. On warm days the pools heat up and evaporation increases the salinity of the water. Cooler weather may bring rain that dilutes the salt water with fresh. Add to this the thousands of shore birds looking for a seafood meal, not to mention human predators. And if all of these difficulties can be overcome there is a final challenge to face; the returning tide. On a calm day it will creep in gently but when the sea is stormy the shore takes a battering. Cold water pounds in bringing with it a hail of pebbles and sand. Taking all of these factors into account it is difficult to understand how anything can survive such a hostile environment. Yet for thousands of creatures the edge of the sea, and particularly the rocky shore, is the perfect place to call home.

The most famous rock pool in the Channel Islands, the Venus Pool in Sark. Named and immortalised by the Victorian artist William Toplis, this natural bathing pool is refreshed each day by the tide.

Rocky Shores

As the tide falls the Islands more than double in size and dozens of square miles of rugged lunar-like landscape are revealed. For the rock pool enthusiast there is no better place to explore armed with nothing more than a net, a bucket and a set of tide tables. The distribution of wildlife on the shore depends entirely on its ability to cope out of the water. Some seaweeds can loose ninety percent of their moisture and still survive. Channelled Wrack lives at the very top of the shore only submerged by the highest tides. For several days it may not even get wet but instead stays curled up, brittle and dry, reviving only when the sea eventually reaches it. A tiny sea snail has also adapted to live in this region high up on the shore. The Small Periwinkle lives in rocky cracks and crevices emerging to feed on lichens. Amazingly it can 'breath' air, unlike other sea snails, and so survive for days out of water. In the breeding season it lays its eggs once a fortnight when the spring tides reach far enough up the shore to make the Small Periwinkle a creature of the sea once again.

Growing up to 27cm long, the Giant Goby Gobius cobitis easily lives up to its name. A rare fish found only in the extreme south-west of the British Isles, it lives in rock pools high up the shore and seems happy to tolerate brackish water.

With its tough shell and robust shape the Limpet is perfectly designed for life high up the shore. When the tide is out it clamps down firmly creating a seal between its shell and the rock which keeps the animal inside cool and moist. Once underwater the Limpet moves across the surface of the rock grazing low growing seaweeds and secreting a trail of slime which it follows to return to its base. In places with softer rock the limpet is able to create a circular 'home' depression by wriggling its shell to form a perfect fit. The hard granite of the Channel Islands makes this impossible so it is the Limpet shell that is ground down to fit the rock. These familiar shellfish were once valued as a food source but few bother to collect them now even though they are plentiful. When it comes to reproduction, the humble Limpet undergoes an astonishing transformation. The younger, smaller individuals are males. As they grow they change sex and live the rest of their life as females. The two do not mate as such but when tidal conditions are favourable thousands of eggs and sperm are released simultaneously and the resulting larvae take their place in the ocean as one of the components of plankton.

Further down the shore the cover of seaweed increases. Spiral Wrack is next then those species with bladders, pockets of air that buoy up the fronds when they are under water. The Flat Periwinkle feeds on these seaweeds and is frequently found in great number. Its colour varies from dull brown and green to bright yellow and orange and it is thought to resemble the air-bladders of its food source. This middle area of the shore is also where some of the most colourful topshells live. The Purple Topshell is beautifully marked with a zigzag pattern and has a very distinct umbilicus, the hole in the centre of the base of the shell. Those without the hole are a rarer species, Pennant's Topshell, found only around the Channel Islands and the Atlantic coast of France and Spain.

Lower down the shore Serrated Wrack takes over, easily identified by its saw-toothed edges, along with Thong Weed which forms long strands growing from the centre of a stalked button. Finally come the largest seaweeds, the Kelp or Oar-weeds, which form a dense forest extending several metres beyond the low tide mark. Exposed only on the lowest tides, its fronds can reach over four metres in length and are often home to the tiny Blue-rayed Limpet. Growing no larger than a thumb nail, this delicate shellfish is marked with iridescent blue stripes and feeds by grazing on the kelp. Like the larger shore-based limpets it forms a 'home base' and the small oval depressions it makes can be found on the kelp fronds washed up on the shore in autumn.

This is very much a simplified account of the most common seaweeds but there are many other varieties thriving around the Channel Islands. A survey in Guernsey alone revealed over 270 different species. The Islanders have a single name for them all: *Vraic*. In the past the huge piles washed up on the shore were a highly valuable commodity and the rights to gather vraic from certain areas were carefully allocated. Living seaweed too was cut on the lowest tides and it was not unknown for quarrels or even violent clashes to break out among the collectors. Spread directly on the land it makes an ideal fertiliser and, once dried, an effective fuel. Iodine can be obtained from the ash of burnt vraic and in the 1920s a factory on Lihou, an island off Guernsey, produced a great deal. At that time it was much in demand as the only effective wound dressing of the day. Many of the beautifully-made granite slipways still in use around the Islands were originally built to allow a horse and cart access to the beach where the seaweed was gathered with big wooden rakes. Nowadays artificial chemical fertilisers are easier to spread on the land but some farmers still take their trailers to the shore to gather seaweed. Much of it though is left to rot on the beach, its pungent smell making it unpopular with some residents and visitors who often demand its

Above: Not found on the shores of mainland Britain, the Pennant's Topshell Gibbula pennanti *is one of several species of topshell found in the Islands.*

Left: At first glance the rocky shore can seem a barren world but the number of sea creatures recorded on the Islands' shores reveal this to be far from true. There are over one hundred species of fish, eighty species of worm, one hundred different crustaceans and an amazing one hundred and sixty species of mollusc.

The seaweed collectors, or Vraitcheurs, *may have forsaken the horse and cart but they still appreciate the value of this free and entirely organic fertiliser. Many Islanders say they can taste the seaweed in the best of the new potatoes.*

The Slipper Limpet or Boat Shell Crepidula fornicata *reproduces rapidly, often at the cost of other shellfish. The population in northern France is estimated to exceed one million tons.*

removal. These less than fragrant mounds, however, are home to bugs and grubs and flies of all description making them a valuable source of food for many of the Islands' birds. This banquet continues even through the winter when the rotting weed generates warmth which keeps the insects alive during the coldest months of the year.

In the 1980s a new seaweed, Japweed, began appearing in the waters around the Channel Islands. It was first recorded ten years earlier in Southampton Water where it was thought to have arrived from the Pacific with cargoes of oysters. It has now spread along both sides of the English Channel and thrives in shallow coastal waters and rock pools. Japweed dies down in winter but from early spring grows with remarkable speed until some of the fronds are over a metre long. Densely branched and covered with tiny, round air bladders and leaf-like fronds, it forms thick tangles which smother smaller, less vigorous seaweeds and Eel Grass. Attempts at eradication on the British coast have been foiled by the Japweed's profusion of spherical reproductive parts which readily break off and float away on the tide, spreading the invasive alien still further. Wakame, another Japanese seaweed, has been growing in some in the Islands' harbours and marinas since the 1990s. Fears that it too would spread and out-compete local seaweeds have so far been unfounded. Should it ever begin to flourish in open water it could always be harvested and served as a delicacy, as it is in Japan.

It is not only exotic seaweeds that have made themselves at home in the seas around the Channel Islands. Slipper Limpets are shellfish that originally travelled to the south coast of England from their North American home in the 1880s as stowaways in sacks of oysters. They quickly spread and made themselves very unpopular with shellfish farmers and fishermen by competing for the same planktonic food as oysters, clams and mussels and smothering these other bottom-dwelling sea creatures. Unlike most other molluscs, adult Slipper Limpets can not move around so have developed an unusual form of reproduction. They form curved 'chains' with each shell clamped snugly on top of another. The individual at the base will be attached to a pebble or another seashell. As the first to arrive, it would have matured as a female then secreted a chemical to attract other Slipper Limpet larvae. The next to settle would attach itself to the female's shell, mature as a male and fertilise her eggs. The chain builds with a female at the bottom and males piling up on top. They live for several years but eventually the original female will die leaving the next limpet up clinging to her empty shell. He will change sex to become a she and the chain continues with as many as thirty Slipper Limpets in a clump. The number of these fascinating shellfish in the waters around the Channel Islands is not known but in places masses of them are washed up on the seashore, many still clinging together in their breeding clusters.

Apart from the lush swathes of seaweed and the most conspicuous seashells the rocky shore can appear quite barren yet a few minutes spent among the rock pools

The thumb-sized coralline algae Corrallina officinalis *thrives in the shallow waters of the rocky shore. The closely related encrusting species Crustose corallines can be seen 'painting' the rocks pink in the background.*

A patch of orange in a rocky crack or encrusted around seaweed is Shredded Carrot Sponge Esperiopsis fucorum. *The large pores that release the water after the animal has filtered out its food are clearly visible.*

reveals a world teeming with life. Many of the pools are lined with what looks like knobbly pink paint. This is a type of red seaweed, described as coralline, that takes calcium from the water and forms a chalky crust on the rocks. On a hot summer's day patches left out of water for any length of time get bleached white by the sun. Another coralline algae forms tiny, pink tree-like tufts which combine with the myriad shades of green and brown of the other seaweeds to make each pool a perfect miniature garden. Sponges often add another splash of colour. One of the most common varieties on the shore is the Shredded Carrot Sponge which forms an orange encrusting sheet from which volcano-shaped cones protrude. In very calm conditions, such as in a harbour, the same species grows long tassels, hence its common name. Sponges belong to the animal group Porifera, which literally translates as 'pore bearer' and includes the tropical species which are dried and used in the bathroom. They are covered in a network of holes through which they draw in water. This is filtered for particles of food and expelled through the larger pores. They have no circulatory, nervous or digestive systems, but are still classed as animals, albeit simple ones.

The Shore Crab Carcinus maenas *is often called the Green Crab although its mottled colours vary from dark green to red-brown and the juveniles can be almost white.*

The Hermit Crab Pagurus bernhardus *only has shell on its claws and head and has to rely on empty seashells to protect its soft body. As it grows it has to move up the property ladder and find larger accommodation.*

The most numerous rock pool residents are the Common Prawns. Although small they deserve to be looked at closely for they really are beautiful creatures. Almost transparent and marbled with fine red patterns their legs are striped with turquoise and yellow. A serrated horn protrudes between the iridescent, stalked eyes. They are never still but constantly flicking their elegant antennae and hopping from leg to leg as if dancing on the spot. Some will dart around in the open, camouflaged against the sand, while the gentle sweep of a small net beneath the weed will reveal plenty of others. You are likely to catch another common crustacean, the Shore Crab, in the same way. Tolerant to air, this crab is able to survive out of water for long periods of time hiding under seaweed or buried in the sand to avoid hungry gulls. Like all crustaceans its soft body is protected in a tough suit of armour which it must shed periodically to grow. This complicated process begins when the crab forms a leathery coat beneath the outer shell. The old carapace splits along the rear and the crab eases itself out backwards, carefully extracting all its limbs, eyes and tiny mouth parts from their old casing. The discarded shell is easily mistaken for a dead animal until the opening at the back is seen. The crab's new leathery shell is now fully exposed and immediately the wrinkly skin begins swelling with water, expanding and hardening. Along with a larger casing the crab will have begun to regrow any limbs lost since it last changed shell. This is a dangerous time for the crab because, as well as its usual predators, it would make an easy meal for a larger crab. Because of this the moulting process is a secretive business and the crab stays well hidden until the new shell is hardened.

The Velvet Swimming Crab Necora puber *is arguably the most aggressive animal in the seas around the Channel Islands. Here the larger male is guarding the female below him until she sheds her shell and is ready to mate.*

In some crabs changing shell is the stimulus to reproduce. When the female Velvet Swimming Crab is about to shed her old shell she releases a chemical signal called a pheromone into the water which tells the male she is about to become fertile. Once he has located his potential mate, the male embraces her from above and guards her from rival suitors. He helps her climb out of her old shell and carefully turns her over so that their bellies are together for mating. Like all crabs she has a special flap under her shell to carry the eggs which she will do for several months until they hatch. A handsome animal with bright red eyes and vivid purple markings, this crab is impossible to mistake for any other species. Known in the Islands as a Lady Crab, and considered a delicacy, it is easily the most aggressive animal living on the seashore. When encountered it will raise up and brandish its claws rather than scuttle away and is quite capable of delivering a painful nip.

One of the largest crabs in the Channel Islands is the Edible Crab, or *Chancre* as it is more commonly known locally. Confusingly it is also called the Guernsey Crab although it is just as abundant in the other Islands. With its thick brown shell, pie-crust edging and dark pincers it is easy to distinguish from other crabs. Small individuals are found on the shore but the largest live in deeper water. The same is true of the Lobster, that other staple of the local fishing industry. Both are caught in baited pots and the tonnage of lobster alone taken from the waters around the Islands amounts

Young Edible Crabs Cancer pagurus *can often be found in rock pools but the largest individuals live in deeper water. Scavengers, they feed on a wide variety of food and in areas of soft sediment will excavate surprisingly large holes in search of shellfish and worms.*

Individual Lobsters Homarus gammarus *have been caught weighing up to 10kg and, at that size, could be up to sixty years old. Those encountered on the shore are likely to be much smaller.*

to more than half that taken from around the coasts of England and Wales put together. For centuries the local fishing industry has depended upon the plentiful supply of crustaceans and, despite the large numbers taken, it continues to be big business. Originally pots were made of willow and were raised and lowered manually and, being fairly fragile, were used only in summer. With the development of tough plastic and steel pots, mechanical winches and sophisticated navigation aids, fishing is now a year-round business with some boats able to fish a thousand pots per day. Restrictions have been imposed on the type of traps that can be used and the size of the animals taken, essential to protect the valuable stocks. The island of Sark takes these measures a step further and allow their waters to be fished for only six months a year.

Like many fish it is the male Tompot Blenny Parablennius gattorugine *which guards the eggs. Even without a nest to defend this little fish has a belligerent nature and will bite a finger if one is offered.*

Like all small brown fish found on the seashore the Shanny Lipophrys pholis *is often known locally as a Cabot. The commonest fish of the rock pools, it is able to survive the trauma of life between the tides.*

When it comes to the fish life likely to be encountered on the seashore many of the hundred or so species found around the Islands can be found in the rock pools. Some are juveniles of those that normally live in deeper water and others have adapted to live soley in the shallows. One of the largest full time rock pool residents is the Tompot Blenny, a red-brown fish with prominent eyes and lips, easily distinguished from similar species by the pair of tassels on its head. A smaller fish with greener colouring and no tassels is likely to be a Shanny. With slimy skin and no scales the Shanny is very difficult to get hold of, an advantage for any animal living on the shore. It too has the ability to survive out of water for several hours if caught out by the tide and can sometimes be seen high and dry wedged into a shaded crack waiting for the water to return.

The Shore Clingfish Lepadogaster lepadogaster *lives attached to the undersides of rocks and in summer its eggs are likely to be nearby.*

To find the most interesting animals on the rocky seashore it is essential to turn over a rock or two. The effort involved is amply rewarded by the treasure-trove of marine life to be discovered underneath. Care must obviously be taken to return the rock to its original position but the creatures revealed are unlikely to be harmed by a brief disturbance. The Shore Clingfish thrives in this environment and, as its name suggests, has a circular fin on its belly which enables it to cling to the undersides of rocks and so lessen its chances of injury in the surge of the shallows. Finger-sized and a deep red-brown colour, it has two bright blue spots on the back of its head and a pair of fringed tentacles on its nose. A less obvious fish is the Worm Pipefish. About the same length as the clingfish but much duller in hue, this little animal really does resemble a worm at first glance. Closer inspection reveals a distinct elongated head and a turned up nose, both of which show its close relationship to the seahorse.

A tiny, lobster-like animal that shoots away as you lift a rock is likely to be a Squat Lobster. There are several species living around the Islands. Most are dull green-brown but one species is bright red with vivid blue stripes. All have flattened bodies

With its flattened body and claws the Broad-clawed Porcelain Crab Porcellana platycheles *is perfectly designed for living in narrow places. A similar, hairless species also thrives in the same environment, the Long-clawed Porcelain Crab* Pisidia longicornis.

Its small size, short blunt arms and almost pentagonal shape make the Cushion Star Asterina gibbosa *impossible to confuse with any other starfish. It is also the only species of starfish commonly found on the sea shore.*

and claws, an adaptation from the normal lobster shape for a life spent in the narrowest cracks and crevices. Another crustacean perfectly designed for living in such confined spaces is the Broad-clawed Porcelain Crab. With a carapace no larger than a little fingernail this crab is covered in bristly hairs and several will be seen scuttling along the underside of most rocks lifted. It shares its world with a small starfish, the Cushion Star. Like the Limpet this little animal has an interesting approach to reproduction. Up until the age of four it is a fully functional male then it changes sex and lives the rest of its life as a female.

The Star Squirt Botryllus schlosseri *a complex colony of tiny animals. It grows attached to rocks or, as illustrated, on seaweeds.*

There are many other creatures living under the rocks, some not easily recognisable as animals at all such as sea squirts. They appear in a range of different shapes. Some form erect tubes or spheres while others grow in encrusting mats which can easily be mistaken for sponges. All are basically a cylindrical, jelly-like body with two openings. One opening siphons water into the animal's stomach where food particles are filtered and digested. The used water is then expelled through the second opening. Sea squirts live either singly or fused together to form colonies such as Star Squirt, the most common species found on the shore. Each of the tiny 'flowers' is an individual animal. Amazingly in their larval form all sea squirts have a primitive kind of backbone making them one of our closest relatives in the sea.

Rocky Shores

The walls of the Gouliot Caves in Sark are carpeted with anemones. It is one of the few locations where Beadlet Anemones Actinia equina *occur together in their three different colour forms of red, orange and green.*

Anemones also flourish in the shallows were sea meets land. Related to coral and jellyfish, anemones consist of a central column, containing the digestive cavity, with a mouth on top surrounded by a ring of hollow tentacles. The Beadlet Anemone is the most common species on the shore, probably because it can survive out of water for so long. When uncovered it pulls its tentacles in completely and secretes a layer of slime to protect itself against the drying air. When the water returns the seemingly lifeless blob of jelly blossoms as the tentacles unfurl and the ring of bright blue 'beads' that give the animal its common name are revealed. Although it appears to be fixed in one place, the Beadlet Anemone is remarkably mobile underwater. It moves in slow motion around the rocks in search of food and will even fight another anemone that comes into its territory using its battery of stinging cells to fend off an invader. By far the greatest concentration of these, and many other anemones, can be found in the Gouliot Caves in Sark. The caves experience the same powerful tidal currents as the nearby and infamous Gouliot Passage between the headland and the island of Brecqhou. The huge volume of water constantly surging through the cave brings with it a blizzard of plankton. The walls are lined with thousands of anemones, along with sponges, hydroids and soft corals, all taking advantage of the abundance of food. This stunning display of colour has quite rightly earned the cavern the charming name of the Jewel Caves.

Unable to completely withdraw its tentacles, the Snakelocks Anemone Anemonia viridis *is often left high and dry on the lowest tides and has to rely on a layer of mucus to survive.*

The spongy yellow balls left on the strand line look like some form of man-made material but are actually the egg cases of the Common Whelk Buccinum undatum. *The first tiny whelks to hatch use the other eggs as food.*

The mysterious green blobs that appear on the seashore in spring belong to the Green Leaf Worm Eulalia viridis.

Rocky Shores

In more open locations yet another anemone can be found on the rocky shore. The Snakelocks Anemone has long, elegant tentacles and comes in two distinct colour schemes. Some are a dull grey-brown while others are bright green with vivid purple tips. The latter coloration is caused by the presence of microscopic green algae that live within the tissues of the tentacles. The algae is able to photosynthesise, that is, produce food directly from sunlight. This adds to any sustenance the anemone can catch with its sticky tentacles and explains why it prefers to live in brightly lit places rather than in the shade. Unusual among anemones it is unable to totally retract its tentacles so, if caught out by the tide, hangs limply from the rocks or sprawls forlornly across the sand. The tiny prawn that lives in Snakelocks Anemones in deeper water is absent from those that live in the shallows. (see page 119 in chapter 5). Maybe the prawn cannot survive the trauma of life on the shore.

In late winter and spring many animals on the rocky seashore begin to reproduce. Close inspection of the undersides of rocks and in cracks and crevices will reveal rows of tiny, pale yellow flasks, the egg cases of the Dog Whelk. More obvious are the egg capsules of the much larger Common Whelk which produces papery masses about the size of an apple. These are formed of hundreds of hollow compartments, each containing up to a thousand eggs. Less than three percent of these develop leaving the rest as a food source. As the hatchlings grow they feed on each other finally emerging as tiny but fully formed miniatures of their parents. Another prominent egg mass belongs to the Green Leaf Worm which can sometimes be seen creeping over the rocks when the tide is out. It leaves gelatinous, pale green blobs of eggs about the size of a marble attached to seaweeds and pebbles.

About the length of a hand, when fully grown the Sea Hare Aplysia punctata *is the largest of its kind in north-west Europe. Related to the snails, it has a much reduced internal shell hidden by its soft tissue.*

Wildlife of the Channel Islands

In late spring the Sea Hare, a large marine slug, prepares to reproduce. Each individual is a simultaneous hermaphrodite, that is it possesses both male and female organs. Unable to fertilise themselves they often form mating chains where each behaves as a male to the one below it and as a female to the one above. They lay sticky strings of eggs that look like tangles of boot laces. In some years there are population explosions of these curious animals and many are washed ashore still clasped in their mating embrace. When disturbed they eject a deep purple ink that is thought to deter predators and which was once used as a dye.

The shell of the Ormer Haliotis tuberculata *has a series of holes. The five closest to the edge are open and the older ones gradually close up as the animal and its shell grow. The animal's sense organs protrude through these holes which it also uses to discharge waste and, depending on its sex, eggs or sperm.*

Once valued for its decorative shell, the Ormer is now sought after only for its meat. Trials are under way on the south coast of England to farm the valuable shellfish but the slightly lower water temperatures on the other side of the Channel prevents them from breeding any further north than the Channel Islands.

Rocky Shores

By far the most popular and well known resident of the rocky shore is the Ormer. A close relative of the limpet, its name is derived from *oreille de mer,* French for 'ear of the sea'. The Islands represent the most northern extent of its range with the slightly lower temperatures on the other side of the Channel deterring its spread to the mainland. A grazer of red seaweeds, the Ormer has been gathered on low water around the Islands for centuries and the lowest tides are still called *Ormering tides*. Many gardens and walls are decorated with the empty mother-of-pearl-lined shells, once exported by the tonne for inlay work in furniture and musical instruments. These days the Ormer is most highly prized as the central ingredient in Ormer stew, a real Channel Island speciality. Tradition dictates it is braised for many hours with onions and carrots, a process that softens the otherwise rubbery seafood. In the 1960s divers in Guernsey collected and exported many thousand Ormers and are said to have made a huge impact on the population. Stern fishing regulations now restrict the times and size at which the Ormer can be gathered in all the Islands and fines can be imposed for even possessing them outside these dates. Gatherers can work from above water only and have to reach under rocks and turn over boulders. The wearing of any underwater equipment such as a snorkelling mask or even swimming goggles is forbidden. In the 1990s a viral infection wiped out huge numbers of Ormers around Jersey but fortunately it did not spread to the other Islands. The local Fisheries Department imposed a total ban on ormering for three years to give the stocks chance to recover, a strategy which seems to have been successful.

Turning over kelp-encrusted rocks on the lowest tides of the year is back-breaking work but many locals consider it well worth the effort for a 'feed' of Ormers.

Shore gathering for all sorts of sea food, not just Ormers, has been a tradition in the Channel Islands for hundreds of years. Special tools have evolved such as wide nets for trawling up prawns and a fork, called a *grapin,* for raking the sand for shellfish. 'Spiking' is still practised, whereby a fisherman has a pole in both hands each bearing two thin barbed spikes. As he wades through the water he stabs the sand hoping to spear a flat fish or two. Some fishers lay out nets or baited lines at low tide, both practices now limited to certain areas and times of the year. Reaching under rocks with some form of hook is the preferred method for catching Lobsters and Edible Crabs and, even though many forms of low water fishing seem to be dying out, the best sites, known as marks, are still closely guarded secrets.

Oyster tables are a familiar sight on the shores of Herm, Guernsey and Jersey. The mesh sacks have to be shaken regularly to prevent the shellfish from fusing together, arduous work for the local oyster farmers whose crop is underwater for much of the day.

Others have taken low water fishing a step further and actually farm areas of the seashore. Oysters are grown in mesh sacks attached to low-lying metal tables. The smallest Oysters are least able to cope with being out of water so are kept furthest down the shore, accessible only on the lowest tides. As they mature they become more tolerant to air and are moved to tables higher up. From the air the large areas covered by the farms are revealed yet from the ground the tables are unobtrusive and often not even seen until you almost trip over them. Filter feeders, oysters open and close with the rhythm of the tide and continue to do so even when exported thousands of miles away. In these nutrient rich waters they take less than three years to mature, the fastest growth rate in the world. Farmers in Jersey alone produce over two hundred tonnes of Oysters a year. Mussels too are farmed and, like the Oysters, no chemicals or fertilisers are used, making them a truly organic crop. The greatest difficulty facing these farmers is that for more than half of the day their 'land' is underwater. Aquaculturalists in Guernsey are now perfecting the art of hatching out tiny oysters and clams and are exporting the juvenile shellfish, known as spat, all over the world.

Like the Red-necked, Slavonian and Black-necked Grebe, the Great Crested Grebe Podiceps cristatus *does not breed in the Channel Islands but spends the winter here feeding close to the shore. It is an agile aquatic hunter able to travel great distances underwater in a single breath (MD).*

A relative newcomer, the Little Egret Egretta garzetta *is now much at home on the shores of the Channel Islands. With the longest legs of all local waders it is able to feed in the deeper rock pools so does not have to compete directly with the other shore birds (MD).*

Wildlife of the Channel Islands

With so much marine life thriving on the rocky shore, it is not surprising that many birds are attracted to the edge of the sea. Herring Gulls, by far the commonest seabird in the Islands, are particularly adept at flicking up the seaweed to catch the crabs that hide beneath. Oystercatchers chisel shellfish off the granite outcrops and many other waders roost on the highest rocks when their feeding grounds are covered by the tide. But one bird has specialised exclusively in hunting in rock pools and is perfectly suited to life as the ultimate low water fisher. With its long legs, sharp eye sight and spear-like beak the Little Egret is able to catch even the best camouflaged fish. Unknown in the Islands until the early eighties, this exotic newcomer is spreading from further south and is now well and truly established in the Channel Islands. In 2002 it even began breeding here. It is the most elegant of birds with gleaming white plumage and delicate crest but the chic image is ruined by a close up glimpse of its feet. Large, bright yellow and clumsy in appearance, they seem to belong to an altogether less refined-looking bird. All is explained if you watch the Egret's hunting technique. It wades deep into the pools and often reaches under the weed with its feet to flush out a potential meal. Crabs also favour these shady hiding places and, with even the smallest able to deliver a powerful nip, the Little Egret certainly needs such heavy-duty footwear.

St Ouen's Bay, Jersey

A typical Channel Island reef. The walls are encrusted with Red Fingers soft coral Alcyonium glomeratum *and Pink Sea Fan* Eunicella verrucosa *as well as a carpet of smaller hydroids, sponges, anenomes and bryozoans (CW).*

Chapter Five

Beneath the Waves

Beneath the low water line the seas around the Channel Islands are home to a wealth of wildlife even more intriguing than that found between the tides. Off the south and east coasts of Jersey the water is shallow, rarely deeper than twenty metres, but to the north and east around the other Islands it drops off more steeply. Many of the cliffs in Guernsey, Alderney and Sark plunge down to fifty metres or more. Further north again lies Hurd Deep, the remains of an ancient riverbed that was all that separated England from the Continent eighty thousand years ago. Almost two hundred metres deep, the trench has been used as an ammunition dump for decades.

As on land, the topography of the seabed around the Islands varies enormously, each terrain supporting a distinct group of wildlife. Dense beds of Eel Grass, like underwater meadows, provide a nursery ground for many species. Shingle banks, forever shifting in the tide, conceal flatfish and rays perfectly camouflaged on the golden seabed. Above them shoals of Sand Eel glitter in the dappled sunlight then vanish in a flash with the approach of a hunting seabird.

The shingle seabed, however, is not always the safest refuge for here lie the grand masters of disguise, Cuttlefish. Surprisingly Cuttlefish are molluscs, like slugs and snails, but when it comes to intelligence this branch of the family leaves the others standing. Along with its close relative the Octopus, the Cuttlefish has an enormous, well-developed brain, the largest of any invertebrate. Other characteristics of this group are the jet propulsion system, for extremely fast getaways, and the internal shell that controls the animal's buoyancy by adjusting the amount of gas it contains. Excellent eyesight teamed with lightning speed and a strong parrot-like beak make it a formidable hunter capable of taking fast-moving prey or well armoured animals such as crabs. To confuse potential predators the Cuttlefish releases a cloud of ink, a highly concentrated form of melanin, which irritates the predator's eyes and temporarily paralyses its sense of smell.

The Cuttlefish also has an incredible facility to alter both the colour and texture of its skin, an ability it employs for camouflage and communication. While hunting over sand it nestles into the seabed, matches its colour exactly with its surroundings and

Living for just two years the Cuttlefish Sepia officinalis *feeds by day and night and will tackle prey almost as large as itself.*

With its well developed eye and enormous brain the Cuttlefish Sepia officinalis *is one of the most intelligent invertebrates, an honour it shares with its close relative the Octopus.*

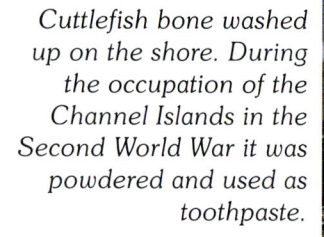

Cuttlefish bone washed up on the shore. During the occupation of the Channel Islands in the Second World War it was powdered and used as toothpaste.

flattens its skin, rendering it virtually invisible to passing prey. Should it move to an area of seaweed it instantly changes colour and tassels form on its skin to mimic the texture of the weeds. During courtship the use of colour is at its most impressive. A male Cuttlefish will ripple with zebra-style stripes, its skin flickering with iridescent patterns and colours. Sacs of pigment in the skin called chromatophores expand and contract to create this astounding display used as much to warn off rivals as to attract a mate.

The female Cuttlefish, though less impressive visually, has an amazing ability of her own when it comes to the mating game. If her eggs are not ready to be fertilised she can store her partner's sperm, conveniently delivered in a sealed parcel, for days or even weeks until she is ready to use it. In the meantime if rival suitors mate with her they first use their water jet to literally blow the previous male's deposit out of her body. Laying the two hundred or so eggs takes the female several days. Each egg, the size of a grape, is laced with her ink and attached to something solid on the seabed. Two months later the fully formed young emerge with all the feeding and colour changing abilities of their parents. This instant self-sufficiency is vital as the adults are rarely still alive by the time the eggs hatch. So much energy is expended during reproduction that they begin to decompose and survive only a few weeks after mating. Their flesh falls away and their familiar Cuttlefish bones, actually the internal skeleton, are washed up on the shore.

The Octopus used to be extremely common all around the Islands until it perished in the exceptionally cold winter of 1962-63 when the shallow margins of the sea froze over. In recent years there have been occasional sightings and the number brought up trapped in lobster pots seems to be gradually increasing. Maybe the 'devilfish' of Victor Hugo's *Toilers of the Sea* will stage a comeback.

Like all jellyfish the Compass Jellyfish Chrysaora hysocella *is closely related to anemones and corals. Sense organs located around the bottom of its bell enable it to stay upright in the water.*

Scallops Pecten maximus *reproduce when they reach three years old. Both the meat and the roe, known as coral, are considered a delicacy.*

    Another mollusc that is still thriving in the waters around the Channel Islands is the Scallop, although it is difficult to see any similarity between this shellfish and the fast-moving Cuttlefish and Octopus, all members of this diverse group of animals. Much sought after in local restaurants, Scallops are fished by two completely different techniques. Dredges dragged behind a boat plough into the seabed forcing the scallops into a heavy chain sack. Small rocks and boulders are overturned and any ground dwelling animals such as sponges, anemones, starfish, Ross Coral and even juvenile Scallops are smashed by the dredge leaving great scars on the seabed that take years to recover. In complete contrast Scallop fishing scuba divers barely touch the seabed and take only the adult shellfish leaving the rest of the marine life totally unharmed. In recent years some divers have taken this process a step further in an experimental scheme called 'ranching'. Protected tracts of seabed are assigned to each diver who in return seeds the area with juvenile Scallops, called spat, that are large enough to be harvested some three or four years later. Some of the spat are eaten by Netted Dog Whelks in their early days and others simply swim away but initial results indicate that enough stay put to make it a viable and non-destructive method of producing seafood. If all fishing techniques were as sympathetic as this there really would be plenty more fish in the sea.

A Mermaid's Purse, the egg sack of the Common Dogfish Scyliorhinus canicula here attached to Fan Coral. The single juvenile will eat its way out five to eleven months later, depending on the water temperature. The empty cases are often washed up on the shore.

With its purple-tipped spikes and large size the Spiny Starfish Marthasterias glacialis is impossible to mistake for any other species. Its voracious feeding habits make it particularly unpopular with Scallop fishermen.

Wildlife of the Channel Islands

As well as people, the Scallop has another equally deadly predator, the Spiny Starfish. A giant in the starfish world this five-armed hunter grows to be over two feet across feeding on shellfish, crustaceans and even other starfish. Scallops are a favourite meal but take some catching. As soon as they sense the first touch of the Starfish's arm they jet away by away clamping and releasing their two shells in rapid succession to propel themselves through the water to safety. For the ones that don't get away death is a slow process. The two halves of the shell are prised apart by the Starfish's powerful arms that can exert a pulling force equivalent to five kilograms. A crack between the two shells as tiny as one tenth of a millimetre allows the starfish entry as it extrudes its stomach out through its mouth and into the gap. Once inside its powerful digestive juices begin to dissolve the soft tissues and the Scallop's fate is sealed. Knowing that they feed on Scallops fishermen have been known to rip the arms off Spiny Starfish should any be bought to the surface, little knowing that, like all starfish, they have remarkable powers of regeneration. Not only can the central body regrow any lost limbs but even a single arm can produce a whole new starfish.

Above: The colonial anemone Parazoanthus axinellae, *another species found more commonly in the Mediterranean that thrives on the rocky reefs around the Channel Islands.*

Right: Jewel Anemones Corynactis viridis *carpet the walls of the deeper reefs in a patchwork of colour.*

The shingle banks where starfish roam are punctuated with outcrops of granite reef topped with a swaying crown of kelp. This canopy of lush plant life provides a home for a whole range of wildlife in much the same way as a forest on land does. Below the kelp, as the light grows dimmer, an entirely different type of life smothers the rock as animals replace plants. Marine biologists call this the circalittoral zone. Sponges, hydroids and bristly bryozoans jostle for space while great swathes of wall are painted with Jewel Anemones in every conceivable colour combination. Like many anemones, these little gems can reproduce by budding clones of themselves if they are living in particularly favourable conditions enabling them to quickly colonise large areas. They may look like delicate flowers but their tentacles are armed with a battery of stinging cells, a deadly trap for any small creature that ventures too close.

Welcome guest or parasite? The true relationship between the Anemone Prawn Periclimenes sagittifer *and its host Snakelocks Anemone is not yet known.*

One animal has found a way of living with this danger, even using it to its own advantage. The Anemone Prawn is another of the Islands' southern species not found around the mainland of England to the north. It lives among the tentacles of the Snakelocks Anemone and appears to be immune to its host's stings that are fatal to other small creatures. Whether this is a mutually beneficial arrangement is unknown although the Anemone can thrive, as many do, without the lodger. The Prawn, however, has never been seen living apart from the anemone. It may even be that the Prawn feeds on the Anemone, a theory supported by the suspiciously similar shade of purple found on the Prawn's body and the tips of the Anemone's tentacles.

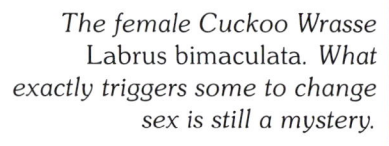

Wildlife of the Channel Islands

The female Cuckoo Wrasse Labrus bimaculata. *What exactly triggers some to change sex is still a mystery.*

A fish with a colourful past, the male Cuckoo Wrasse Labrus bimaculata *wouldn't look out of place on a tropical coral reef.*

    One of the commonest fish on the deeper reefs is the Cuckoo Wrasse, an inquisitive animal with the most remarkable sex life. The female is fairly distinctive with her rosy-pink body and bold black and white band but the male is positively exotic. Resplendent in his vivid orange and blue livery his colours seem almost luminescent in the watery half-light of the reef. The colour difference between the sexes is so extreme that they were once thought to be two separate species. Living with a harem of females the male attracts their attention by blanching his head pure white, a signal also used to warn off rivals. But life for a Cuckoo Wrasse is complicated for all are born as females. Between seven and thirteen years old some undergo an amazing transformation. Brighter colours appear on her nose and her black and white marks fade. As the sex change progresses she becomes a fully functional he and may live to be at least seventeen years old. Exactly what sparks this alteration is unknown and many females live all their lives without transforming. It may be the loss of the harem's resident male that triggers the oldest female to change sex to replace him, a reaction seen in some tropical fish. Whatever the reason the Cuckoo Wrasse remains the most dazzling fish in the Channel Islands.

Smaller than the average thumb, the Sunset Coral Leptopsammia pruvoti *makes up for in beauty what it lacks in size.*

Of all the animals that live attached to the reef, the most conspicuous are the corals. These waters are home to at least nine different species and, while they might not grow as large as their tropical cousins nor build vast reefs, they are just as colourful and, unfortunately, just as fragile. Closely related to sea anemones, coral is made up of polyps, a mouth surrounded by stinging tentacles which catch water-borne food particles. Some are solitary, known as cup corals, and live independently although there are often many others nearby. At first glance cup corals look like small anemones but closer investigation will reveal a hard vase-shaped structure made almost entirely of calcium carbonate out of which the colourful tentacles blossom. The most dazzling of the cup dwelling species is also the rarest, the Sunset Coral. Extremely slow-growing, this animal is thought to live for over a hundred years and is another southern species more commonly found in the Mediterranean.

A close up of the soft coral Red Fingers Alcyonium glomeratum *reveals the polyps with their eight tentacles that catch particles of food to feed the whole colony.*

The other Channel Island corals live in colonies, a mass of polyps joined together to form one growth such as Dead Man's Fingers. This is a soft coral, which has no hard skeleton but grows as a flexible, gelatinous mass supported by tiny calcareous threads from which the polyps protrude. When feeding the fingers are upright and the multitudes of tiny mouths open wide to catch particles of food turning the vertical rock faces where they thrive white and fluffy. As the tide slackens the corals rest, the polyps withdraw and the fleshy fingers droop down. Maybe it was in this state that they earned their gruesome name.

Although the nudibranch Tritonia nilsodhneri *feeds exclusively on the Sea Fan. The polyps they eat seem to regrow so that the entire coral is not killed. The photograph shows two individuals coiled around branches of the coral with a ribbon of their spawn in the top right.*

The Pink Sea Fan is the most recognisable of all the corals living in these waters. It grows in a branching pattern like a miniature tree and is formed of a flexible, horny substance called gorgonin. Reaching out across the prevailing tidal flow so that the polyps can feed, it is easily damaged by clumsy scuba divers or badly placed fishing gear. Despite its name the Pink Sea Fan is variable in hue and the different colour forms seem to have a regional bias. Whereas those on the north side of the English Channel are normally pink, around the Islands both pink and white forms occur, and in southern Europe and the Mediterranean they are all white. With a growth rate of just one centimetre a year the largest fans can be over 70 years-old. Many of the Islands' sheer reef walls are embellished with these beautiful corals giving the chilly waters of the English Channel a truly tropical feel.

Grazing among the corals in this underwater animal garden are the sea slugs, or nudibranchs to give them their proper name. Closely related to the slimy pests so unwelcome in the garden, marine slugs are incredibly elaborate and colourful creatures. The term nudibranch literally means 'naked gill' and refers to the animals' exposed gills which either form a cluster near the rear or are arranged as tentacles all over the

Unmistakable with its rings of short bobbles rather than tentacles, the Imperial Anemone Aureliania heterocera disappears below the seabed with incredible speed if disturbed.

Measuring little more than two centimetres across its body, the Scorpion Spider Crab Inachus sp. is tiny. It is pictured here on the sponge Axinella dissimilis.

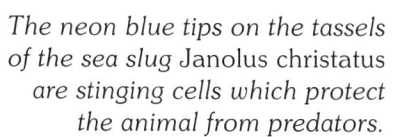

The neon blue tips on the tassels of the sea slug Janolus christatus are stinging cells which protect the animal from predators.

body. Most are very small, often thumb-sized or less, and very few have common names. The scientific name, however, is frequently rather grand once translated. *Janolus cristatus*, the nudibranch illustrated, is described as a crested two-headed Roman god named Janus. Quite a title for a tiny slug.

All nudibranchs are carnivores and many have the ability to digest the stinging cells of their prey, such as anemones, without triggering the tiny weapons then use them for their own defence. They are all simultaneous hermaphrodites, that is they possess both male and female sex organs, which makes finding a mate twice as easy. While some can be found on the shore most live beneath the low tide mark so it is scuba divers who stand the best chance of admiring them to the full. Spring is the prime slug-spotting time for by the middle of the summer most have mated and died, investing their future in delicate ribbons of eggs.

The male Lumpsucker Cyclopterus lumpus *is a dedicated father which guards his developing offspring until they hatch. The mass of eggs is clearly visible in the bottom right of the photograph.*

Spring is a busy time for the natural world and the marine creatures of the Channel Islands are no exception. As the days lengthen and the water slowly begins to warm all sorts of fascinating fishy courtship activity is triggered. First on the scene is the Lumpsucker, a knobbly, rugby-ball-shaped fish with large, fleshy lips. Normally a deep water resident, the male, flushed pink and orange with his breeding colours, lumbers into the shallows as early as February. He clears a patch of rock to form a nest and settles down to wait for the female. A circular fin on his belly acts as a sucker holding him firm in the surge. Much larger and duller, the female Lumpsucker duly arrives staying only long enough to lay over a hundred thousand eggs. Left alone the male guards the eggs blowing and wafting with his fins to keep them clean and oxygenated. He is fiercely protective of the nest and chases away any predators intent on a tasty snack of lumpfish roe. It's a dangerous two months for the dedicated father. He does not eat and is an easy target for seagulls at low water. The tide itself brings the greatest danger, particularly with the huge rise and fall in the Channel Islands, and many are fatally washed ashore in the late winter storms.

A male Corkwing Wrasse Crenilabrus melops *putting the finishing touches to his nest, the mass of seaweed to the right of the photograph.*

The next drama to unfold features the Corkwing, one of six species of wrasse found around the Islands. Once again the male fish is the colourful one with his dull greens and browns marbled with iridescent blues and reds in the spring. To further impress a mate he goes to great lengths to build an elaborate nest which is often wedged in a crevice in the rocks. Day after day he swims to and fro selecting the best pieces of seaweed for his construction and carefully weaving his watery bower. Swollen with eggs, the female is further enticed by an intricate courtship display, all flashing fins and gaping mouth. Once wooed she lays her eggs and again the male is left to guard them until they hatch. But this love story has an intriguing twist. Some young males prefer not to build a nest of their own. Instead they have the colourings of a female misleading nest building males into allowing them access to the nest where they fertilise any eggs already present. Drag queen fathers, a truly fishy business.

The male Black-face Blenny Tripterygion delaisi *in full breeding colours.*

Another fish with a penchant for showing off to attract a mate is the Black-face Blenny. A southern species, these little fish are a rarity on the northern side of the English Channel but fairly common around the Islands where they live on steep rocky walls. By early summer the male's orangey-brown body has turned bright yellow, his head is almost black and his fins are trimmed with bright, electric blue. He dances around his mate in a figure of eight pattern flicking his fins as if to make sure she admires him from every possible angle. In comparison the female's colours are so dull as to render her almost invisible against the rock face and her presence is often only revealed by the wriggling motion that signals her readiness to mate.

The male Dragonet Callionymus lyra *displaying his stunning breeding colours to a potential mate.*

But when it comes to attracting the opposite sex there is one little fish that surpasses all others. For much of the year the Dragonet is a drab, mottled brown creature easily overlooked on the sandy seabed where it lives. In early summer though the male, much rarer than the female, develops shimmering turquoise stripes and spots dramatically outlined in black. He darts around possible mates pausing to flaunt an elaborate dorsal fin spanning the full length of his back and arching forward beyond his nose. He may only be the length of a hand but this little fish means to be noticed and, as courtship displays go, he could give a peacock a run for his money. Although there is no shortage of females, the males still compete and the sight of them trying to outshine each other is a miniature spectacle worthy of any coral reef let alone the cold waters of the English Channel. Once satisfied with her choice of mate the female swims to his side. Trembling against each other the Dragonets move along the seabed then up into mid-water where they spawn leaving their fertilised eggs to be carried away on the tide. Instantly they dash back to the sand where the male immediately begins displaying to another potential partner.

Later on in the summer the sea is home to yet another display of fascinating natural behaviour. In July Spider Crabs gather by their hundreds to shed their shells. Why they prefer to moult en masse is unknown but perhaps there is safety in numbers. In the shallows these congregations often gather against a rock face or harbour wall, as if the crabs favour having their backs protected, while at sea great moulting mounds are formed. In either case the Crabs move to the bottom of the pile to shed their shells. Empty carapaces frequently float to the surface and are washed ashore in great numbers often sparking fears of some disaster in the Spider Crab population as the discarded shells are mistaken for dead crabs.

Popular with fishermen, the Tub Gurnard Trigla lucerna *loses its brilliant colours when taken out of the water and by the time it dies is almost white.*

The John Dory Zeus faber, *aptly described as looking "like a dinner plate with fins". Legend has it that the dark spot in its centre is St Peter's thumb print left when he took money from the fish's mouth.*

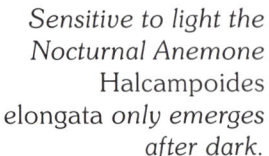

Sensitive to light the Nocturnal Anemone Halcampoides elongata *only emerges after dark.*

After the sun goes down the marine version of the night shift takes over and, particularly in late summer when the water is at its warmest, the sea can be busier after dark than it is by day. Hunters that have stayed hidden all day emerge from the darkness to feed. Lobsters leave their holes and march across the seabed in search of food, dead or alive and will even eat each other if the chance arises. Flatfish and rays surface from their sandy hiding places to forage and the bright red Tub Gurnard scours the seabed for a meal. Specially adapted feelers reach out from the beneath its colourful pectoral fins like fingers on which it appears to walk along the bottom. These taste-sensitive tentacles probe into the sand for food. Tub Gurnards often feed in a small group who communicates with a series of eerie grunts that carry a surprisingly long distance underwater. The John Dory is another expert hunter very active by night. Its flattened shape means that front on it's almost invisible allowing it to get within striking distance of smaller fish before its protrusible jaws are shot out to engulf the ill-fated prey.

Triggerfish Balistes carolinensis *often move into Channel Island waters in late summer but even then it is not warm enough for them to breed.*

The John Dory is not the only exotic-looking creature in these waters. Every year there are regular sightings of Turtles and Sunfish and, after the warmest weather, Triggerfish appear, late summer visitors from much further south. Their strong lips and sharp teeth are perfectly designed to crack the hard cases of the crustaceans and shellfish they feed on but there is one thing these tough fish cannot cope with; the cold. As the sea cools they must return to warmer climes to survive and the bodies of those that do not are tossed up on the shore in late autumn. Their skin is so thick and tough that the usual seashore scavengers can not get to the flesh beneath so the Triggerfish are washed up whole.

When it comes to marine mammals the Channel Islands are particularly well blessed. Long-finned Pilot Whales are often seen around Guernsey and Sark and there are occasional sightings of Minke and Fin Whales. Harbour Porpoises and Risso's Dolphins have also been recorded and Common Dolphins are regularly seen feeding on shoals of Mackerel or Bass all through the year. They tend to favour the deeper waters around Guernsey where schools of up to one hundred have been seen. The shallower waters

The Long-finned Pilot Whale Globicephala melas *is actually a member of the dolphin family and feeds almost entirely on squid (TR).*

Bottle-nosed Dolphins Tursiops truncatus *live in schools of up to thirty and are found in all but the polar seas. Born after twelve months gestation the calves stay with their mothers for up to three years before they can fend completely for themselves.*

off Jersey are home to Bottle-nosed Dolphins. Like many of their kind they seem to be attracted to boats and will ride the bow wave of any vessel from the smallest fishing boat to the big cross Channel ferries. They are most often seen off the south and east coasts and are one of only four resident populations in the British Isles.

The dolphins are by far the largest residents in the seas around the Islands but even they are dwarfed by the occasional visit of a real giant, the Basking Shark, the largest fish in European seas. Growing up to ten metres long it eats nothing but plankton, minute floating plants and animals, filtering over a thousand tonnes of water an hour while feeding. Swimming close to the surface with its huge mouth wide open it is an impressive sight, one most likely seen on the calmest of summer days.

Weighing up to seven tonnes and feeding only on plankton, little is known about the life history and biology of the Basking Shark Cetorhinus maximus.

Finally, there is one type of marine environment that cannot go unmentioned. The Islands have a rich maritime heritage the story of which is written on the seabed in the rusting remains of shipwrecks. From the Romans to the Elizabethans and on to the heyday of steam and the grim traffic of two World Wars, the treacherous reefs and tides have claimed their victims and continue to do so today. To add to this, since 1993 the island of Jersey has been creating a number of artificial wrecks by cleaning up old ships and barges and sinking them under controlled conditions. However the ships, or even aeroplanes in a few incidents, end up on the seabed man's misfortunes are readily claimed by the sea and soon transformed into living reefs of iron.

Wreck of the Striker *a small fishing boat off the north coast of Jersey. Whether deliberately sunk or the result of a tragedy, shipwrecks provide a haven for marine life.*

First to arrive are those organisms swept along as planktonic larvae, particularly in the spring and summer when the water is laden with such life. Keel worms, barnacles and sea squirts can grow even on the smoothest surfaces and give other slower-growing species something to hold on to. In this way animals such as anemones, sponges and corals that rely on the water currents to bring food get a toehold and quickly flourish. A Dutch cargo vessel sunk in the second World War off the south-west corner of Jersey is smothered in Oatenpipe Hydroids, a sort of stalked anemone. The overall effect is to give the ghostly outlines of the old ship a friendlier, fluffy appearance. Shoals of silver and bronze Pouting hang like curtains around this and many of the other sunken ships earning them their alternative name of wreck fish.

Pouting Trisopterus luscus *often shoal around the Islands' wrecks earning them their other title of wreck fish. Quite where the additional local name of 'flobber' came from is unknown.*

The sheltered insides of a wreck where there is little water movement tend to be much barer and often rather silty. But these areas are not without their life as dark holes like these provide the ideal home for the notorious Conger Eel. In the past the Islands were famous for their catches of these giant eels which were exported all over Europe. In 1694 a Jerseyman, Phillipe Falle, wrote, "But the sea about this and the adjoining islands might be titled the kingdom of the congers, so great is the quantity taken". Conger stew decorated with marigolds was a popular local dish in the past when fishmongers used to sell the Eels door-to-door from wooden barrows.

Much maligned with a fearsome reputation, the Conger Eel Conger conger *is shy and docile underwater unless threatened.*

The conger's culinary popularity may have declined but its fearsome reputation has not, stemming from both its ferocity when caught and the fact that it can still deliver a hefty bite after many hours out of water. To be fair to the much-maligned Eel any animal fighting for its life will lash out and a powerful, muscular creature that feeds on fish and crustaceans is likely to have sharp teeth. Underwater it is a docile, even timid creature unlikely to attack unless provoked or threatened and often seen sharing its hole with Common Prawns. Why the Conger does not eat the prawns is unknown but it is possible that they clean the Eel as some tropical prawns do in warmer waters. The Prawns in return are protected by the sheer presence of their large live-in bodyguard. Like all eels the Conger's biology is somewhat mysterious but they are known to migrate to deep water spawning grounds in the tropical Atlantic where the female lays several million eggs. So much energy is expended in reproduction that, like Cuttlefish, the adults breed only once then die soon after.

The Short-snouted Seahorse Hippocampus hippocampus *is rarely seen but this may have more to do with its superb camouflage than its rarity.*

A fish with a completely different approach to reproduction is the Short-snouted Seahorse. In common with tropical species of seahorse the male and female of this mythical-looking creature are thought to court each other with a ritual dance that can last for days. Eventually the female lays her eggs in a pouch on the male's belly where they are fertilised and so ends her part in raising the young. For the new man of the fish world the work has only just begun. His pouch seals over to protect the developing brood that he nourishes with oxygen and possibly a hormone found in nursing mammals called prolactin. Several weeks later the tiny, perfectly formed Seahorses are expelled from the pouch by vigorous contractions. Although less than a centimetre long the young are able to fend for themselves and, like their parents, feed by sucking tiny crustaceans through their tube-like snout.

Little is known about seahorses in British waters. Indeed it is only in recent years that their presence has been recognised as anything but accidental, summer visitors swept in on warm currents from much further south. A survey in the Channel Islands in the late nineties showed them to be present here all year round, from the tiniest juveniles to fully grown adults. Not so much tourists as fully qualified residents, but what was really surprising was where they were discovered. Most of the records were from lobster fishermen who found them either clinging to pots or on the deck of the boat after the pots had been raised. Assuming the Seahorses attach themselves to the pots on the seabed it seems they are living at well over thirty metres and, in the case of some records from Guernsey, as much as sixty metres deep. Other sightings have come from shallow, weedy areas and rock pools, more 'traditional' Seahorse habitats. There is even a well-documented colony thriving among the fuel film, noise and detritus in one of the new marinas. Even more surprisingly there are no records at all from the Eel Grass beds which does not necessarily mean they do not live there. With chameleon-like colour-changing skills Seahorses have an incredible ability to blend with their surroundings and are easily overlooked.

Seahorses turn up in the most unexpected places. These juveniles were found in the stomach of a large pollack.

In 2002 an angler off Sark made another interesting Seahorse discovery when he caught a large Pollack in deep water south of the island. For its last meal the unfortunate fish had dined on Seahorses with over a dozen inch-long juveniles left undigested in its stomach. Not only do records like this confirm that Seahorses breed here but they indicate their presence in some number. Around the world millions of dried Seahorses are consumed annually in the Chinese medicine and marine curio trades and, because of the difficulty of feeding them live food with enough nourishment, thousands more starve to death every year in captivity. At a time when, internationally, Seahorses are under such threat, populations such as these in the Channel Islands must be cherished and protected.

Several wet meadows in Jersey and Guernsey are protected for the wealth of orchids they contain. The Loose-flowered or Jersey Orchid Orchis laxiflora is generally the tallest and is a continental species not found on the British mainland.

Chapter Six

The Interiors

Away from the coast and the immediate influence of the sea, the interior of the Channel Islands consists mainly of open countryside with varying amounts of residential areas. Freshwater habitats are limited to a mixture of natural and manmade ponds and reservoirs, some small streams and the few remaining marshy areas. In Jersey, Guernsey and Sark the land is intersected by steeply wooded valleys that run down to the sea. Agriculture has shaped the landscape for over five thousand years since Neolithic man first began to clear the forest for his crops and live in settled communities. Historical records from Plantagenet times suggest that, in Jersey at least, corn was the main crop. In the seventeenth century cider became hugely popular and great swathes of farmland in the two larger Islands were planted with orchards. By the beginning of the nineteenth century small, mixed farms were the norm. The difficulty of transporting fresh produce from either the British mainland or the Continent meant that the Islanders relied on home-grown produce as their only source of crops. This self-sufficiency became even more essential when the war between France and England left them in constant fear of siege and invasion. This agricultural history has left its mark on today's countryside and, although some hedges have been removed to accommodate modern farming techniques, many fields are still very small by current north European standards.

The flamboyant petals of the Common Poppy Papaver rhoeas *are shed after a single day. Modern farming techniques have all but eliminated it from corn fields but it is still a familiar sight on roadsides and waste ground where its seed can remain dormant for years until disturbed and provoked into germination.*

Flowers, fruit and vegetables became important crops from the middle of the nineteenth century as trade links with England were strengthened. The Islands' southerly position and relatively mild climate meant that farmers could deliver their produce that much earlier than mainland growers and cultivate more slightly 'exotic' crops. Guernsey began specialising in growing under cover and built glasshouses to supply grapes to the London market. From around 1870 potatoes and outdoor tomatoes became important crops in Jersey and Guernsey. Potatoes, particularly the early varieties, are still a significant crop and huge areas of agricultural land are covered in plastic sheeting in late winter to promote their early growth. From the air the shiny plastic gives the impression that much of the land lies under water. Even steeply sloping fields, known as *côtils,* are farmed, especially those facing south. The tiniest patches of this valuable land are planted and, particularly in fields too small or steep to allow the use of a tractor, much of the work is done by hand. Every year the growers gamble on being able to get their potatoes to market early enough to earn the premium that pays for such a labour-intensive crop. Occasionally they are caught out when an unseasonably hard frost ruins the harvest.

The Islands' hedgerows and waste ground are a living museum of old Daffodil varieties where their bulbs have been dumped after becoming no longer commercially viable.

The Interiors

In Guernsey many farmers specialised in growing crops indoors and early in the twentieth century acres of glasshouse were constructed to cultivate tomatoes, cucumbers and other tender produce. Vast amounts of vegetables were exported at the peak of this trade. In 1957, for example, more than nine million trays of tomatoes were sent to England. Towards the end of the century the economic climate shifted when growers could no longer compete with cheaper imports from European Union countries. Some turned to the cut flower trade while others dismantled their greenhouses or simply let them fall into disrepair. Today Jersey and Guernsey still grow flowers, indoors and out, although this industry, too, has declined in recent years. From late winter onwards fields of cultivated Daffodils and Narcissi can still be seen striping the landscape with their various shades of yellow. Just as many thrive in hedgerows, neglected fields and on wasteland where the bulbs have been dumped or abandoned. Dozens of these varieties exist in the wild reflecting the fickle nature of the flower business where a bloom may be the height of fashion one year and a commercial disaster the next. Jersey also has the true Wild Daffodil, or Lent Lily, which is smaller than the commercial hybrids. It thrives in wooded valleys, and on the cliffs where bracken grows up to shade the bulbs from the summer sun as they finish flowering. They reproduce by seed so grow as individuals rather than in clumps like the mostly infertile commercial varieties the bulbs of which multiply below ground.

Like the Guernsey, the Jersey Cow is much tougher than she looks and can be found all over the world. In the Channel Islands a few of the smaller herds are still tethered to individual lines pegged to the ground where they graze the lush grass in their own personal crop circles.

Livestock farming has also been extremely important to the economy of the Channel Islands. Small numbers of sheep and pigs are still raised and Guernsey claims its own breed of goat, the Golden Guernsey. Without a doubt though it is the cattle that the Islands are best known for throughout the world. Both the Jersey and Guernsey cow give incredibly rich, creamy milk with high levels of butterfat. Their herd books were introduced by the middle of the nineteenth century marking the official creation of the breeds which are thought to have their origins in the cattle of the near European Continent. Docile and delicate in appearance, both breeds are actually quite hardy. They are able to maintain their high yields in extremes of climate from the harsh winters of Canada and Scandinavia to the heat and diseases of the tropics. They have been exported all over the world to create new herds or to interbreed with local cattle to improve their yields. These days live animals rarely leave the Islands but instead their genes are exported as 'straws' of semen for artificial insemination. Alderney, too, had its own distinct breed of dairy cattle. Slightly smaller than the Guernsey but with an even higher butterfat content in her milk, the breed was sadly lost in the Second World War. The few cattle that remained in Alderney during the German Occupation perished while those that were transported to Guernsey beforehand were mixed with local cattle. By 1945 the Alderney as a separate breed had ceased to exist. It is immortalised in a few old photographs and the poem, *The King's Breakfast*, written in 1924 by A A Milne.

Two common butterflies of the open countryside. The Comma Polygonia c-album (right) is a master of disguise with its ragged silhouette providing excellent camouflage and caterpillars that look like a bird's dropping. The Orange Tip Anthocharis cardamines (left) flies from April to early June and is most likely to be seen along roadsides, ditches and damp meadows where its food plants of the cabbage family grow.

The Interiors

When it comes to wild mammals the Channel Islands vary from each other quite considerably, a result of human intervention and of the time difference between each Island's isolation from the Continent. Red Foxes were briefly introduced to Jersey, possibly more than once, where the last one was shot at the end of the nineteenth century. Badgers have never lived in any of the Islands. Rabbits were brought over in the Middle Ages and kept in closely guarded warrens or *garennes*, their meat reserved for the Seignuers, the local nobility. Impossible to contain, the Rabbits escaped and were soon common in all of the Islands. In the mid 1950s the fatal rabbit disease Myxomatosis took a huge toll on the population and was almost certainly deliberately introduced by man. Records from the period in Jersey show that, without the Rabbits' constant grazing, the vegetation on the cliff tops and dunes grew luxuriantly. Initially all of the flora seemed to benefit but eventually the larger, more vigorous plants began to crowd out the more delicate species. Myxomatosis still strikes when numbers become particularly high and the sight of a Rabbit dying a slow death with the disease is not a pleasant one. In recent years Rabbit populations in Jersey and Guernsey have also had to contend with viral haemorrhagic disease, a lethal condition first recorded in domestic rabbits in the 1980s. Interestingly, Alderney and Sark have a number of very dark or black wild Rabbits, possibly as a result of breeding with escaped domestic animals. Another school of thought proposes that this is a natural wild form that survives without the usual grey-brown camouflage due to the lack of Foxes that would otherwise pick off such conspicuous prey. Whatever their colour, Rabbits, particularly young ones, do have their predators in the Channel Islands. Peregrine Falcons will take them and I have been unfortunate to witness a Great Black-backed Gull snatch a young Rabbit from the cliff top. The shrieks of the youngster as it was swept over the sea still kicking were a potent reminder of the brutality of life in the wild.

Not an albino but a fully-fledged blonde. Four decades of breeding from a tiny gene pool has resulted in at least a quarter of Alderney's Hedgehogs having this unusual colouring.

Hedgehogs are another introduced species and were released in Jersey and Guernsey around 1850 with a few recorded in Alderney at the end of the same century. The Alderney Hedgehogs did not fare as well as those on the larger islands and had all but disappeared by the end of the First World War. In the 1960s, however, two or more pairs were introduced to act as four-legged garden pest controllers. One of the pairs came from Harrods department store in London while the others emigrated from Guernsey. Decades of interbreeding has allowed the spread of a rare recessive gene with the result that at least a quarter of Alderney's Hedgehogs are very pale brown in colour and described as blonde. Scientifically speaking they are *leucistic*, which is a colour form in its own right rather than an absence of colour. This can clearly be seen in their eyes which are very dark brown rather than the bright pink of an albino. Another interesting characteristic shared by all of Alderney's Hedgehogs is that none of them carry fleas. The human residents have very much taken the 'Blondies' to their hearts and, featuring on stamps and postcards, they are as much a symbol of Alderney as the Gannet and Puffin. In Sark Hedgehogs are a little less popular. They were released in the 1980s, again with the intention of providing a natural pest control. Instead their taste for eggs and chicks has been blamed for a noticeable decline in the number of ground nesting birds within a few years of their arrival. Since the end of the 1990s an unusually high number of Sark's Hedgehogs have succumbed to disease so perhaps their future in the island is less than certain.

Sark, however, does have one claim to fame in the small mammal world of the Channel Islands; it is home to the Black Rat. Infamous as the carrier of the flea that in turn bore the bubonic plague, it is thought that the Black Rat arrived in the Channel Islands in the thirteenth century. This is when it colonised western Europe from its home in Asia, possibly arriving as a stowaway in the Crusaders' ships. Five hundred years later the Brown Rat arrived in Europe. It is assumed that in the Channel Islands Black Rat numbers declined as the Brown newcomers flourished, as they did elsewhere. Now almost certainly extinct in the other Channel Islands, the Black Rat has survived in Sark, and its tiny neighbour Brecqhou, and is considered a rarity in the British Isles. Smaller and slimmer than the Brown Rat, it has a more pointed nose, larger ears and a longer tail. Black Rats are also faster moving and reported to be even better climbers than their Brown relatives.

A description of the smaller mammals living in the countryside again highlights the differences between the Channel Islands themselves and the mainlands between which they lie. All of the Islands have the Long-tailed Field Mouse which, although the same species as its mainland counterpart, is larger and more brightly coloured. Its pale brown coat and bigger eyes and ears distinguish it from the grey-brown House Mouse which lives in all of the Islands except Herm. Jersey alone is home to the Bank Vole and Guernsey has the Field Vole. Over the centuries these isolated island

The Interiors

The French Shrew Sorex coronatus, *also known as Millet's Shrew.*

With its pale plumage and heart-shaped face the Barn Owl Tyto alba *is impossible to mistake for any other owl. Renowned for its eyesight, it relies just as much on its remarkable sense of hearing and is able to locate prey by ear in total darkness.*

populations have evolved slight differences from their common forms and both vary sufficiently to have been named as separate subspecies. Shrews live in all of the Islands but the distribution of the three species found here is less than straightforward. The distribution of the Greater and Lesser White-toothed Shrew is described in chapter three, either species but not both being found in all of the Islands. Jersey also has the French Shrew which, as its name suggests, is another continental species. Like the White-toothed Shrews it is equally at home on the seashore and in the countryside. Shrews feed on insects and their larvae and as such are classed as insectivores, rather than rodents, and are therefore more closely related to hedgehogs than to mice and voles. They have short but immensely active lives surviving for little over a year. They breed rapidly producing three or four litters of up to six young in their lifetime. If the nest is disturbed the female rescues her offspring in a characteristic 'caravan' of shrews. The young hold on to the base of each other's tail forming a train with the mother in the front leading the way to safety. Another distinctive feature of most shrews is the musk gland on their flanks. The strong aroma they release when handled may explain why cats rarely eat any shrews they catch. This scent, however, is no deterrent to their greatest predators, the birds of prey.

Kestrels are the most numerous bird of prey in the Channel Islands and are as common in the countryside as they are over the cliffs and coastal heaths. Mice, voles, shrews, small birds and worms provide some of their nourishment and a study of their pellets reveals that beetles also make up a fair proportion of their diet. In contrast the Barn Owl feeds almost entirely on small mammals. A study in Jersey at the end of the twentieth century revealed that Bank Voles are at the top of its menu followed in equal proportion by Long-tailed Field Mice and both species of Shrew. The unmistakable pale bird is the most numerous owl in the Channel Islands although a few Long-eared Owls breed here and a small number of Short-eared Owls occasionally visit for the winter or stop off on migration. Since the 1980s conservation groups have provided dozens of nest boxes for Barn Owls in an effort to compensate for the loss of traditional breeding sites in old buildings and holes in trees. The Barn Owls have readily taken to their new accommodation and their numbers have substantially increased. Their otherworldly shrieks can often be heard in the darkness of the countryside at night and the headlights of a lucky driver may reveal their ghostly forms swooping low over the lanes. In early summer they sometimes hunt by day, driven by the demands of up to seven hungry owlets.

Colourful newcomer or unwelcome pest? The Pheasant Phasianus colchicus *uses its strong claws to unearth potatoes from their ridges making it unpopular with farmers. In spring the breeding plumage of the male is particularly striking making him far more conspicuous than the mottled brown female.*

The Interiors

Without doubt the most conspicuous bird of the open countryside is the Pheasant. Game birds have been introduced to the Channel Islands several times over the centuries. Often they were shot to extinction but on occasion a few survived the guns to breed in the wild. Red-Legged and Grey Partridges for example still live in very small numbers in some of the Islands. The Pheasant is present throughout the Islands but was absent in Jersey until an illegal introduction in 1985 which led to something of a population explosion. While some residents appreciate the exotic splash of colour it adds to the countryside, others are very concerned about the increasing numbers of this alien bird. The Pheasant's taste for new potatoes and other tender vegetable crops has made it unpopular with farmers and gardeners. With no natural predators and an estimated population of over a thousand birds, it is hard to imagine that one species can increase so rapidly without having any detrimental effect on the native wildlife.

Left: From April onwards many of the hedges in the Channel Islands are lined with Three-cornered Leek Allium triquetrum. *Cattle love its juicy leaves and stems but the plant's garlicky flavour taints the milk.*

Below: In May and June large patches of Common Dog-violet Viola riviniana *can be seen along the hedgerows and banks. Although very similar in appearance, it lacks the delicate fragrance of its earlier flowering relative the Sweet Violet.*

Wildlife of the Channel Islands

The network of lanes and tracks that criss-cross the interiors of the Channel Islands are bordered with hedgerows, banks and walls. These provide a valuable natural habitat for all kinds of wildlife including wildflowers. One of the first to brave the chilly days of late winter is the Sweet Violet, a garden escape now naturalised in the hedge banks and woodlands of Jersey and Guernsey. Its white or violet flowers release a heady fragrance which seems to disappear the moment it is detected. This trick of the nose is induced by ionine, a chemical in the flowers' scent that quickly anaesthetises the sense of smell. A minute or two away from the Violet restores the olfactory senses and the flower's perfume can be enjoyed again, if only briefly. Lesser Celandine, Primrose and Snowdrop also raise their delicate heads early in the year followed by hordes of Daffodils and Narcissi. As the days lengthen Three-cornered Leek, another garden plant now well established in the wild, appears in profusion along the roadsides. Its name refers to the stems which are distinctly triangular in section. Also known as Stinking Onions in some of the Islands, more of its pungent smell is released if its glossy, slightly fleshy foliage in disturbed. Alexanders is another early plant of the hedgerow and the first member of the parsley family to flower. Although it is tall and grows in abundance in many areas, the greenish-yellow tinge of its flowers make it easier to overlook than some of the more colourful wildflowers.

In early May the Jersey Buttercup begins its short flowering period. A real island speciality that grows in a few sites in Jersey alone, it can be distinguished from the common Meadow and Creeping Buttercups by its single flower on a usually unbranched, upright stem and the rosette of leaves at its base. It grows in thin rocky soil and needs to have wet conditions through the winter but be very dry in the summer. One of its strongholds is an outcrop of rock next to a busy main road where it goes mostly unnoticed by the thousands of drivers who pass within touching distance every day.

Found only at a handful of locations in the south and west of the island, the Jersey Buttercup Ranunculus paludosus *grows on steep rock faces with a thin soil covering (RL).*

The Interiors

As spring warms into summer the banks and hedgerows flourish into a canvas of greens splashed with the pinks and purples of Red Campion, Herb Robert and Foxglove. Hogweed and Wild Carrot form billows of creamy-white flowers and Honeysuckle weaves its fragrant peach-coloured blooms among the hedges. In some places garden escapes such as Crocosmia, Pink Oxalis and Gladiolus add their harsher shades of orange, cerise and ruby-red respectively. As beautiful as the summer hedgerows are, the vegetation needs to be cut back to keep the roads and lanes clear. Both the larger Islands have the *Branchage*, an ancient law governing rights-of-way culminating in a ceremonial inspection on set dates in July and September. Any landowner allowing his trees, hedges or vegetation to overhang the road surface below a set height is fined. The penalty is aimed to be less of a financial forfeit and more of a source of public embarrassment for the offender. The severity of the July trim in particular may seem brutal but it comes at a time when most of the wildflowers have set at least some of their seeds. It may also keep down the coarser grasses, hogweeds and brambles that might otherwise take over.

Left: The Jersey Fern Anogramma leptophylla, *one of the Islands' specialities, grows on almost vertical stony hedgebanks that are damp in winter but dry in summer (RL).*

Right: Wall Pennywort Umbilicus rupestris *is widespread on the walls and banks of all the Channel Islands. Its other common name, Navelwort, and the first part of its scientific name refer to the dimple in the centre of each leaf.*

Above left: Ivy-leaved Toadflax Cymbalaria muralis *is a south European plant originally brought to the Islands for garden rockeries but now thriving in the wild on walls and stony banks.*

Above Right: Red Valerian Centranthus ruber *flowers from May to September and, despite its name, can be dark red, pink or white.*

Mexican Fleabane Erigeron kavrinskianus *was first recorded growing wild in the British Isles in the capital of Guernsey hence its other common name of St Peter Port Daisy (RL).*

The Interiors

The stony banks and granite walls that add so much character to the Islands' rural and urban landscapes support wild rock gardens that far outshine those planted by human hand. Many are dappled with crusts of orange or pale green lichen and those in damper locations harbour all manner of mosses and liverworts. Spleenworts and other ferns grow in the crevices and those with a keen eye for botany may find one of the three Guernsey hybrids or the Jersey Fern. Far easier to identify and much more widespread is Wall Pennywort. The shiny, circular leaves are present all year round and in June its tall spikes of greenish-white flowers begin to bloom. It grows from a tuber which, along with its fleshy leaves, stores moisture so that the plant can survive the heat and drought of summer. Ivy-leaved Toadflax is also well adapted for life on stone walls. Originally a garden plant, it forms swags of green foliage dotted with tiny, snapdragon-like purple flowers. Once these have been fertilised the stem bearing the seedhead shies away from the light, curling into the darkness of crevices and planting its capsule in the cracks of the wall. The surface of the seed is ridged, a characteristic that helps it stay wedged in the best place to germinate.

There are two other very conspicuous plants that thrive untended on the walls of the Channel Islands; Red Valerian and Mexican Fleabane. Both were originally introduced as garden flowers. Like many of the plants that grow on walls, Red Valerian has long tap roots that bury themselves deep in the crevices between the stones to anchor the plant and seek out moisture. Its sweet scent attracts butterflies and other long-tongued insects which can reach the nectar at the base of the tube-shaped flowers. The seeds are topped with a hairy parachute that carries them away on the wind. Mexican Fleabane is a member of the daisy family and grows almost exclusively on walls. It forms stunning swathes of flowers which are at their most spectacular from April to October, although it blooms almost all year round. As the flowers age they become tinged with pink and are nearly purple by the time they shed their petals.

A description of the wildlife on the walls of the Islands would not be complete without mention of the Wall Lizard. Another continental species, small numbers of these beautiful little reptiles have been introduced to southern England but there are three well established colonies in Jersey. Smaller and less brightly coloured than the Green Lizard, close inspection of the Wall Lizard reveals intricate cream and brown patterns on its olive-green skin. Used to human activity, with a little patience it is possible to get very close, particularly early in the mornings when the Lizards bask in the sun to warm up for the day's activities. In common with most lizards they have the ability to autotomise, that is they can release their tail if they are grasped by it. This gives the lizard the chance to escape, a technique further enhanced by the tail which wriggles for some time after breaking off, further distracting the predator. In time a new tail will grow back but it often lacks the colour and length of the original.

The Wall Lizard Podarcis muralis *is found in and around three historic sites in Jersey. When the walls of the buildings are repaired care is taken to ensure that plenty of lizard-sized holes are left between the stones.*

Felled for fuel during the shortages of the Second World War and blighted by disease and storm damage later in the twentieth century, the tree population of the Channel Islands has faced some difficult times in the last decades of the millennium (RP).

The Interiors

As with much of the plant and animal life, the variety of trees in the Channel Islands is an interesting mixture of northern European species and those from much further south. The salt-laden westerly winds do not provide the ideal growing conditions but there are a number of sheltered, well watered valleys with thickly wooded sides and some trees are left to grow in the hedgerows. Even Alderney, sometimes mistakenly described as treeless, has some patches of woodland and Herm too has its own area of trees. Oak, Sweet Chestnut and Ash are common in the Islands' woods and there are small numbers of Pines. Being fairly salt-resistant Escallonia and Euonymus are commonly used in hedges as are Hazel, Holly, Elder, Hawthorn and Blackthorn. In marshy areas and by streams Common Sallow and other Willows have been planted. Sycamore is one of the commonest trees in both hedgerow and woodland but its ability to self-seed and its rapid growth rate have made it something of a pest. Originally from the mountainous areas of Central Europe, studies have shown that it harbours around ten percent of the insect and other invertebrate life of the Oak, a typical native tree. The evergreen Holm Oak is also fairly common in the Islands. Originally from the Mediterranean, it grows well in exposed sites on the coast as well as inland. Its presence, however, is not always entirely welcome in the wild because very few plants can grow beneath its dense canopy of leaves. Tamarisk is another introduced species which thrives in the salty, windswept margins close to the sea. It has been planted for hedging and forms feathery shrubs or small trees that turn pink in midsummer as its dense clusters of tiny flowers bloom at the ends of its twigs.

The tiny, scale-like leaves of the Tamarisk Tamarix gallica *help the shrub retain moisture in the dry habitat it prefers. Its resistance to salt water made it a favourite among Guernsey fishermen who used it to make the base of their lobster pots (JM).*

Wildlife of the Channel Islands

Elm Trees are perfectly suited to the Islands' maritime environment and were extremely common until the outbreak of a virulent strain of Dutch Elm Disease in the late 1970s. In Jersey alone it was estimated that over 300,000 trees were lost to the disease and Guernsey's landscape was affected even more dramatically as a higher proportion of its trees and hedging were Elm. These losses are thought to be even greater than the huge number of trees felled for fuel during the German Occupation of the Second World War. The disease is a fungal infection spread by the Elm Bark Beetle which lays its eggs under the tree's bark. As the fungus grows it clogs the tree's water vessels which in effect starve it to death. The Great Storm of 1987 took another huge toll when many thousands of the largest trees were destroyed. Since then Islanders have been replanting trees and hedgerows as well as creating new areas of woodland.

Speckled Wood butterflies Pararge aegeria *are a common sight in woodland glades where they compete for territory and conduct their courtship. The brown-flecked wings are an ideal camouflage in this dappled world of leaves and sunlight.*

The Turtle Dove Streptopelia turtur *is the smallest of four species of pigeon that breed in the Channel Islands. It arrives from Africa at the end of April and nests in tall, mature hedges and on the edge of woodland (MD).*

The Interiors

The Islands' copses and tree-lined valleys are home to a wide variety of common woodland birds. Wrens, Blue Tits and Great Tits are among the most vocal along with Blackbirds, Robins, Chiffchaffs and the occasional flock of Long-tailed Tits. A small number of Spotted Flycatchers breed here in the summer while more are seen during the spring and autumn migrations. Jersey's woodlands provide a breeding site for the Great Spotted Woodpecker although this magnificent black, white and crimson bird is shy and more often heard than seen. The characteristic drumming sound is used by both sexes to proclaim their territory. Each burst of sound is around sixteen blows delivered to a favourite piece of dead branch in less than a second. The Woodpeckers usually carve out a new nest cavity every year, a task that can take up to two weeks. Between three and eight eggs are laid and when they hatch the chicks are fed on caterpillars.

The mature woodlands of the two largest Channel Islands are home to a small brown bird that causes great excitement among visiting birdwatchers, should they be lucky enough to see one. The Short-toed Treecreeper is a continental bird with subtle differences from the species found in Britain. The pale stripe above the eye is less distinct, the bill is slightly longer and, as its name suggests, the Short-toed version has a smaller rear claw. Without the two birds side by side these variations are virtually impossible to see but, as the other species has almost never been recorded in the Islands, it would be safe to assume that any Treecreeper seen here is the Short-toed version. Getting a close look can be difficult for the bird very rarely stays still. It flies to the base of a tree then scurries up the trunk in a spiral, pausing only to snap up the insects it feeds on. At first glance it looks more like a small rodent which explains why it was once known as the 'mouse-bird'.

Along with the smaller birds, many sizeable area of woodland in the Channel Islands contain a pair of Sparrowhawks. Feeding entirely on other birds, this raptor hunts through the trees and over open farmland and occasionally raids garden bird tables, snatching one of the diners with breathtaking speed.

A native of southern Europe, the intricate, hollow form of the Latticed Stinkhorn Clathrus ruber *initially emerges from an egg-like structure that wilts after a few days. Unfortunately its looks are not matched by its smell which resembles rotting flesh to attract the flies that disperse its spores (RL).*

Without having to compete with Grey Squirrels, Jersey's Red Squirrels Sciurus vulgaris *are free to enjoy the hospitality of their human neighbours. About a third of the Squirrel population regularly visit feeding stations and advice is offered to their hosts by the local Environment Department on how to provide them with a balanced diet.*

Jersey's woodlands are home to arguably the most charismatic of all the Channel Islands' wild animals; the Red Squirrel. The exact date of their introduction at the end of the nineteenth-century is uncertain but genetic studies have confirmed that some came from southern England while others were brought over from the Continent. In the 1990s concern grew over the isolation of the various groups of Squirrels in the island. In order to link the patches of woodland they inhabit a programme of hedge and tree planting was initiated so that the groups could mix and interbreed. Rope bridges have been strung across roads and signs erected to encourage drivers to slow down although an alarming proportion of Squirrels still fall prey to traffic. Cats too take a significant toll on the population. Many islanders though have taken the 'Reds' to their hearts and plenty of gardens sport specially designed Squirrel feeding boxes. Research suggests that this supplementary high energy food appears to be extending their breeding season. In Britain Red Squirrel numbers have fallen catastrophically since the more robust Grey Squirrel arrived from North America at the end of the nineteenth century. The Red Squirrel population has been further reduced by disease and now there are real fears for the future of the native Squirrel on mainland Britain. This makes the protection of the Red Squirrel in Jersey even more meaningful. The woodlands here would certainly be duller without the shrill chatter of their calls and the flashes of red fur as they leap through the trees.

The Interiors

A mist-net survey of bats in Jersey in 2002 revealed at least one unexpected result. The bat on the right is the relatively widespread Grey Long-eared Bat Plecotus austriacus *while the individual on the left represents the first Channel Island record of a Brown Long-eared Bat* Plecotus auritus *(FG).*

Described as creatures of 'myth and misunderstanding', bats are naturally woodland animals but in the Channel Islands, as elsewhere, they have taken to sharing human accommodation. Contrary to popular belief they often choose modern buildings, preferring to roost somewhere free from draughts and cobwebs. Grey Long-eared and small numbers of Natterer's Bats breed in the Islands but the commonest residents are the tiny Pipistrelles. Weighing on average a mere five grams, less than a two pence piece, these amazing creatures consume up to three thousand insects in a single night, catching and eating them on the wing. The Common Pipistrelle is most numerous and three other species of Pipistrelle are known to breed here while Greater Horseshoe, Serotine, Leisler's and Brown Long-eared Bats have occasionally been recorded. As daylight fades the bats emerge to feed, flitting at high speed around the edges of woodland, over freshwater and along tree-lined lanes. They also hunt on the seashore skimming above the high tide line and snatching the flies that hover above the piles of seaweed. Human eyes struggle to follow their fleeting movements in the half light of dusk yet the bats' remarkable echolocation can detect the size, shape and texture of the tiniest insect in total darkness.

Yellow Rattle Rhinanthus minor *is a semi-parasitic plant of grasses in moist meadows. Its common name was inspired by the sound of its ripe seeds rattling in their pod but it is also known as the Chick and Egg Plant because the shape of its flower resembles a chick hatching.*

Yellow Iris Iris pseudocorus *flowers from June to August and thrives in damp valleys and marshy areas. Its seeds were roasted and used as a substitute for coffee beans during the extreme food shortages of the German Occupation.*

Ragged Robin Lychnis flos-cuculi *is a plant of wet meadows and marshland. It is closely related to Red Campion but is easily distinguished by its tattered-looking petals (RL).*

In common with much of Britain and Europe, many wet meadows and patches of marshland have been drained in the Channel Islands and much of this precious wildlife habitat has been lost to urban development or farmland. However, some key areas have been protected for the unique variety of plants and insects they harbour. Of the many wildflowers that thrive in these damp areas, it is the orchids that attract the most human attention. They belong to one of the most diverse families of flowers in the world and a little research into their lifecycle reveals each bloom to be a small miracle. The flower produces tens of thousands of seeds that are so tiny they drift like dust in the wind. To germinate and grow the seed has to form an intimate partnership with a soil-dwelling fungi that provides the infant plant with the water and nutrients it needs to develop. It stays underground as a leafless shoot for several years before emerging as a plant. Its flamboyant blooms attract the insects that fertilise the flowers and so continue the complex orchid life cycle.

The tallest and most distinctive wetland orchid in the Channel Islands is the Loose-flowered or Jersey Orchid. Its name in both Guernsey and Jersey-Norman-French refers to Pentecost, an indication of the time of year it flowers. It is another continental species which is not found at all on the British mainland and features on the Jersey ten pound note to the right of the Queen's portrait. Normally rich purple in colour but

Like many orchids the Heath Spotted-orchid Dactylorhiza maculata *has developed a complex method of ensuring its pollination. While a bee or hoverfly is feeding on its nectar, a pollen-covered stamen detaches and sticks to the insect's head and is carried away to fertilise the next orchid it visits.*

The Southern Marsh-orchid Dactylorhiza praetermissa *is easy to confuse with the Heath and Common Spotted-orchids, a mistake made all the more easy by the number of hybrids between these three species.*

occasionally white or pink, the Jersey Orchid is easy to distinguish from other orchids by its well-spaced flowers. The Southern Marsh-orchid, Heath Spotted-orchid and Common Spotted-orchid all share the same habitat but their flowers are tightly packed on the stem. Normally the latter two have spotted leaves but these markings are not always distinct making it difficult for the casual admirer to tell these orchids apart. Such distinctions are made all the more confusing by the hybrids that have developed from these three plants. Knowing the name of each bloom, for me at least, is of little importance, for a swathe of mixed orchids set against the lush green background of a wet meadow is one of the most striking sights in the Channel Islands.

Until the early years of the twentieth century there was another species of orchid living here, one that was prized above all others. Jersey and Guernsey were well known among Victorian botanists for the extremely rare Summer Lady's-tresses, a small orchid with white, almond-scented flowers arranged in a spiral around the stem. Many collectors took specimens from the wild, complete with the plant's tuber, an unsustainable practice which made a huge impact on the orchid's population. It was last recorded in Guernsey in 1914 and Jersey in 1925 and so has long been considered extinct in the Islands, killed by those who treasured it to death. Autumn Lady's-tresses, a very similar and closely related orchid, is still found here. It flowers in late summer and grows in the wild in short turf and in the lawns of gardens and churchyards.

During mating the brightly coloured male Common Blue Damselfly Enallagma cyathigerum *grasps the female by the neck while she curves round to bring her genital aperture into contact with his sperm capsule. The male often stays with her while she cuts a slit in an aquatic plant stem or leaf and lays each egg separately.*

The Southern Emerald Damselfly Lestes barbarus *is a continental species at the north-western limit of its range in the Channel Islands. Like a dragonfly it feeds on other insects and is able to seize its prey in full flight or snatch it off the vegetation (RP).*

The wet meadows, streams and ponds of the Channel Islands are not only valuable for the plants they support but also for the various insects that rely on freshwater for part or all of their life cycle. Without doubt the most colourful and conspicuous of these are the damselflies and dragonflies, an ancient order of insects whose ancestors have been found in fossils dating back some 350 million years. They spend their larval form underwater using their substantial jaws to feed on just about any animal they encounter from other insect larvae to tadpoles and small fish. Damselfly nymphs spend almost twelve months underwater while some dragonfly larvae can take up to five years to complete their development. Both emerge in the summer, crawling out of the water and up the stems of aquatic plants by night or early in the morning. As the shimmering insects heave themselves from their drab outer casings they prepare for life on the wing. This transformation from an aquatic creature to the aerial existence of the adult is made all the more remarkable by the radical respiratory changes the insects must endure to move from life underwater to that in air. There they become voracious aerial predators with remarkable flying skills that will allow them to hover, move forwards, backwards and sideways and change direction with breathtaking speed. Their immediate urge will be to breed for these incredible insects are surprisingly short-lived. Dragonflies survive for up to two months while damselflies can have as little as two weeks to find a mate and reproduce.

Some damp areas in Guernsey are home to an insect that must qualify as one of the most bizarre creatures in the Channel Islands: the Mole Cricket. It uses its powerful, spade-like front legs to burrow up to a metre beneath the ground in search of the plant roots and small soil-dwelling animals such as worms on which it feeds. The male excavates a chamber which amplifies the churring song he performs on balmy

The Interiors

evenings in May and June to attract a female. Once wooed, the female lays her eggs which she tends by licking them until they hatch a month or so later. The nymphs take a year to mature and once fully grown will be the size of a small thumb and covered in chestnut-brown velvety hair. These strange insects were once common in Britain but are now thought to be extinct on the mainland as much of their damp natural habitat has been drained for farming and spoilt by pesticides. Their continued presence in Guernsey is an incentive to protect the remaining damp areas while some scientists speculate that the island's lack of Moles may also increase their chance of survival.

The Mole Cricket Gryllotalpa gryllotalpa *has wings but spends most of its life underground. Damp sandy soil near ponds or drainage channels provides the perfect ground for its extensive excavations (JP).*

The Agile Frog Rana dalmatina *has a more pointed snout and longer legs than the Common Frog. Like all frogs and toads it will return to where it was spawned to breed.*

Wildlife of the Channel Islands

Freshwater is essential to amphibians, as any child who has watched the magical metamorphosis from spawn to miniature frog or toad will tell you. This group of animals again reveals interesting differences between the Islands as well as the continental influence on their natural history. Palmate Newts are found in Jersey while Guernsey and Alderney have the slightly larger Smooth Newt. Outside the breeding season the two are difficult to tell apart but in spring the male Smooth Newt develops a crenellated crest that runs the length of his body and tail. The Palmate Newt grows a much lower crest and develops webs between his hind toes prior to breeding. The females of both species are courted with an elaborate mating display during which the males vibrate their crests and lash their tails from side to side. Frogs and Toads have no such formalities. The male simply grasps the female in an embrace known as amplexus, often while she is still on the journey back to the pool where she was spawned. Guernsey, Sark and Alderney are home to the Common Frog while Jersey has the Agile Frog, a continental species not found on the British mainland. Its numbers have been falling since the 1940s due to the loss or pollution of suitable ponds and predation by cats, Herons, feral ferrets and introduced fish. Newts and ducks have a taste for frog spawn so they too have partly been blamed for the Agile Frog's demise. Towards the end of the twentieth century local environmentalists and the Durrell Wildlife Conservation Trust began working on projects to reverse this decline but the future of the Agile Frog in the Channel Islands is far from certain.

Common Toads Bufo bufo *photographed underwater while breeding. The much larger female may have carried the male on her back for several days and, should he tire, there will be another suitor waiting in the wings.*

The Interiors

The Toad's neat ribbons of eggs are easy to distinguish from Frog spawn which is laid in an irregular clump.

Jersey alone is also home to the Common Toad. Their absence from the other Channel Islands earned the Jerseyman the title of *Crapaud* amongst the other Islanders which is the Jersey-French word for toad. (In the same vein Guernseymen were called *Les Ânes* because of the number of donkeys in St Peter Port.) At the end of February the mature adult Toads gather to breed. Many are killed by traffic as they return to their spawning grounds although road signs have been erected in recent years warning drivers of their presence. The mating call is rarely heard but the males often emit a high-pitched 'qwark-qwark-qwark'. This is known as a release call and, as its name suggests, is made when a male mistakenly embraces another male. In the dark this is an understandable oversight for the females are often totally outnumbered. Each mating pair has several rival males vying for a chance to get to the female and occasionally she is drowned by a surfeit of suitors. Once, while photographing toads breeding, one particularly ardent male attached itself to my lens and it took some force to persuade it to release its amorous grip. In the wild Common Toad numbers are falling but they still seem happy to breed in domestic ponds, a trend to be encouraged both for the Toads themselves and the natural pest control they provide in the garden.

Natural stretches of open freshwater are something of a rarity in the Channel Islands with the largest being La Mare au Seigneur, better known as St Ouen's Pond, in Jersey. Both of the larger Islands have sizeable man-made reservoirs and Guernsey also has a brackish pond at Vale as well as numerous small, deep pools created by quarrying. Alderney too has flooded quarries and there are natural ponds on Longis Common and at Platte Saline. There are no rivers in the Islands but there are plenty of streams. Some trickle over the cliffs forming small waterfalls while most are absorbed in the shingle or sand as they reach the coast. Over the centuries various fish such as

While hunting, the Grey Heron Ardea cinerea *can stand motionless for an extraordinary length of time before spearing its prey with a swift strike of its dagger-like beak. In the Channel Islands it as likely to be seen feeding in rock pools as it is in fresh water, particularly when the tide is out (MD).*

Kingfishers Alcedo atthis *breed occasionally in the Channel Islands but most seen here are passing through on migration or staying for just the winter. Very shy, most encounters with this elusive bird consist of a flash of brilliant electric blue accompanied by its shrill, piping call (MD).*

The Interiors

Carp, Roach, Tench, Bream and Trout have been introduced while Rudd, Stickleback and Common Eels are thought to be indigenous. Herons and Kingfishers are attracted by the fish-life but both birds are as at home on the coast as they are inland. Cormorants are just as adaptable and frequently leave the sea for a spot of freshwater fishing, much to the annoyance of human anglers.

Apart from the ubiquitous Mallard, the Tufted Duck Aythya marila *is the most numerous duck in the Channel Islands. With his striking black and white plumage and drooping crest, the male is easily distinguished from the dark brown female (MD).*

Freshwater, be it open reservoir, reed-fringed pond or stream, attracts all manner of bird-life. The most obvious and easily observed are the ducks, with the Mallard by far out numbering any other species. The male in his splendid breeding colours topped with his iridescent blue-green head contrasts with the drab brown female whose plumage is designed to blend in with the vegetation where she incubates her eggs. Many Mallard living in the wild are hybrids and their domestic ancestry is revealed in strange-looking plumage variations. Interestingly, the classic 'quack' of this duck is made by the female alone; the male only capable of a weak rasping sound. Tufted Ducks come next on the list in terms of numbers. Smaller than Mallards, they feed underwater making as many as a hundred short, shallow dives in an hour. Found in Jersey all year round, Tufted Ducks are seen in the other Islands through the winter and often form mixed flocks with Pochard. Teal, Gadwall, Shoveler and Wigeon also spend the colder months here along with the Little Grebe. Of these winter visitors small numbers of Pochard, Shoveler, Gadwall and Little Grebe sometimes remain to breed. In spring Garganey can be seen on migration while the reeds and rushes provide breeding sites for Moorhen and Coot. Some stretches of water have resident pairs of feral Mute or Black Swans.

The Reed Warbler Acrocephalus scirpaceus *is one of the most numerous warblers breeding in the Channel Islands. Its nest, deep in reed beds, is a favourite among Cuckoos but, fortunately for the Reed Warbler, these brood parasites are rare in the Islands (MD).*

In spring and autumn large numbers of Swifts, Swallows and Martins pass through the Channel Islands on migration and some stay for the summer and breed here. Some of the best places to watch these aerial feeders, whether they are passing through or here for longer, are over stretches of fresh water. Their breathtaking agility while hawking for insects is matched only by their ability to skim the surface and scoop a drink in a meticulously timed low level swoop.

The Interiors

The strident call of the Cetti's Warbler Cettia cetti *is delivered from dense reeds and scrub so the bird is heard but not often seen. Small numbers now breed regularly in the Islands but it was unheard of here before 1960.*

For the shier birds the most valuable areas of freshwater are those with plenty of vegetation around the margins, for the reeds, sedges and willows provide food and excellent cover. During migration Reed Buntings and various species of warbler break their long journeys in the Islands, while spring sees the arrival of those that breed here. Sedge and Reed Warblers announce their presence in April with exuberant bursts of song though a clear view of either of these secretive, small brown birds is a rarity. The same is true of the only resident reedbed warbler, the Cetti's. The male's explosive volley of sound cuts through all other bird song and is distinct enough to leave even the most inexperienced birdwatcher in no doubt of its presence. Named after an eighteenth-century Italian Jesuit, the Cetti's Warbler is a Mediterranean bird that has slowly extended its range northwards. It was first seen in the Channel Islands in 1960 but was not recorded breeding until well into the next decade. Since then they have become well established in Jersey and small numbers have bred in Guernsey and Sark. Like the Dartford Warbler, this diminutive bird feeds on insects and spiders and so is susceptible to hard winters with even short cold snaps proving fatal. Unusually the females far outnumber their mates so each male can have up to three broods at once but takes virtually no part in their rearing.

With a wing span of well over a metre and its slow, gliding flight, the Marsh Harrier Circus aeruginosus *is difficult to confuse with any of the other Channel Island birds of prey (MD).*

In spring 2002 bird watchers scanning the reed beds at St Ouen's Pond in Jersey were treated to a spectacular aerial display as a pair of Marsh Harriers locked talons and tumbled through the air as part of their courtship display. These magnificent birds were no strangers to the Islands having been regularly recorded on migration but none had ever bred here before. Like many birds of prey, the Marsh Harrier was persecuted in Britain and Europe throughout the nineteenth century then, just as its numbers were recovering, the population crashed again in the 1960s due to increased use of persistent pesticides. By the end of the twentieth century it was experiencing quite a dramatic recovery and it was perhaps only a matter of time before the birds discovered the joys of living in the Channel Islands. The male of the pair was thought to be fairly young and possibly not old enough to breed but their courtship continued and nest building began. The pair were successful but their fortunes were followed with mixed emotions by the human observers. The Harriers' taste for other birds raised concern for the rest of the feathered wildlife in the area, particularly the Lapwings which had also just started breeding near the Pond. However, if their table manners can be forgiven, the sight of these magnificent birds of prey soaring effortlessly over the reed beds is a wonderful scene to behold.

Bluebells in Dixcart Woods, Sark

La Grève de la Ville on the east coast of Sark looking north towards Banquette, an ancient landing site.

Chapter Seven

Seeing Wildlife in the Channel Islands

Getting there

There are airports on the three largest Islands, with regular flights from the British and French mainlands and several European cities, although the choice and frequency diminishes through the winter. There is also a regular fast ferry service between the Islands, France and the south coast of England. Sark and Herm are accessible only by sea, with daily crossings from Guernsey throughout the year and some sailings in the summer from Jersey. Alderney has a limited ferry service in the summer to Normandy and Guernsey but if you are travelling from England, unless you have a boat of your own, there is no alternative but to take to the skies. For those who do have their own boat, be it motor or wind-powered, the Channel Islands make a particularly wonderful destination. The rock-infested, tidal waters are not suitable for novice sailors but the view of the Islands, and especially the seabirds, from the water is spectacular. You may even be lucky enough to be escorted on part of your voyage by Bottle-nosed Dolphins or Pilot Whales. There are marinas in Jersey and Guernsey and sheltered moorings in Alderney and Sark. All the Islands have safe anchorages depending on the wind direction.

The ferry arriving in Herm harbour. There are several boats a day from nearby Guernsey which also has a regular ferry service to Sark.

Wildlife of the Channel Islands

When to visit?

Along with the rest of northern Europe, the weather is most temperate in summer although endless sunshine is by no means guaranteed. All the same, this is when many people visit the Channel Islands. The most popular beaches and sun traps are fairly crowded in July and August but, with a little effort and know-how, there are plenty of places to be found in which to be alone with the wildlife. Autumn can be wild with storms one day and warm sunshine the next. This is an excellent time of year for birdwatching as the Islands lie on the main migratory routes of many species. As the days get shorter the first of the birds that stay for the winter begin to arrive from their breeding grounds further north. Winter itself is relatively short and mostly mild. The seashore is alive with waders and gulls but, apart from a few hundred of those, you can have the beaches to yourself. Spring often comes early and in March and April the tide of wildflowers that smothers the Islands through the summer is bursting into bloom. Again migratory birds are on the move and many stop here to rest and refuel. Through May and June the cliff tops and hedgerows are at their most colourful, the seabirds colonies are in full swing and, for me at least, the Islands are at their most glorious.

Seeing Wildlife of the Channel Islands

JERSEY

Jersey has a wonderful variety of natural habitats ranging from unspoilt heathland and sand dunes to steep rocky cliffs and wooded valleys. This, plus the fact that it was connected to continental Europe for much longer than the other Islands, is the reason why it has the greatest diversity of wildlife in the Channel Islands. Many swathes of its countryside are protected but most allow public access with well maintained footpaths and beautifully illustrated information boards. The wildest of all the wildlife areas must be St Ouen's Bay in the west where a dramatic golden storm beach stretches the length of the coast between two sheer granite headlands. The northern end is a rugged cliff-top heath called Les Landes. The acres of low-growing Gorse and Heather are home to Meadow Pipit, Skylark and Stonechat and it is probably the best place in Jersey to see the rare Dartford Warbler. Kestrels and Ravens soar over the cliffs and Peregrine Falcons are also seen regularly. Many migrant birds break their journey

Wild Thyme Thymus polytrichus in St Ouen's Bay. La Rocco Tower, in the background, is one of thirty-one coastal towers built at the end of the eighteenth century to defend the island from French invasion.

here and winter sees the occasional Snow Bunting. The most north-westerly point, Grosnez, is ideal for watching seabirds particularly during the strong westerly winds. Manx, Sooty and Balearic Shearwaters can often be seen passing as well as a variety of Skuas at certain times of the year. On land early spring sees Common Toads congregating in the boggy areas and small ponds to breed and, later in the year, Golden-ringed Dragonflies emerge from their larvae in the shallow streams.

Stretching almost the full length of Jersey's west coast, St Ouen's Bay is a haven for wildlife. Along with the headlands and heaths to the north and south much of it is protected for the valuable flora and fauna it harbours.

Within St Ouen's Bay itself much of the countryside is protected for the valuable wildlife it harbours. La Mielle de Morville, in the northern half, is a stretch of sandy heathland criss-crossed with footpaths and dotted with Common Gorse, Tree Lupin, Rough Star-thistle, Fennel and Evening Primrose. In winter there are flocks of Lapwing and Golden Plover and, in recent years, small numbers of Lapwing have stayed on in spring to nest in nearby damp meadows. There are also several small ponds in this area, one of which is overlooked by a hide for birdwatchers. Now well known for its wildflowers, bird life and insects, it is hard to imagine that until the 1980s much of this land was used as the island's rubbish dump. The interpretation centre housed in nearby Kempt Tower has a mass of information on the area's history and natural history. A little further south and inland is Le Noir Pré, often known simply as the Orchid Fields. In May and June the marshy meadows are a riot of colour as the flowerspikes of four species of orchid and various hybrids unfurl their exotic petals. Other flowers of interest include Ragged Robin, Yellow Bartsia, Tufted Vetch and Square-stalked St John's-wort. Footpaths are carefully mown through the fields in the flowering season so the flora can be enjoyed without being trampled.

Further south again lies La Mare au Seigneur, often simply called St Ouen's Pond, the largest natural area of freshwater in the Channel Islands. The open water attracts all manner of wildfowl including the resident Mallard, Tufted Duck, Moorhen and Coot. In winter they are joined by Shoveler, Wigeon, Pochard and Teal, with small numbers of Little and occasionally Great Crested Grebe. In late spring and summer the air above the water is often alive with feeding Martins and Swallows. The dense reed beds that circle the pond provide a breeding ground for Bearded Tits, Cetti's, Reed and Sedge Warblers, while Herons hunt around the watery fringes. Recently Marsh Harriers have bred here, no doubt fuelled by the great variety of feathered food available. There are two bird hides here, both with views over the water and the reed bed. The surrounding wet meadows and dry grasslands are also protected and provide nesting sites for Skylarks, Meadow Pipits and Lapwing. On warms days Green Lizards bask and stalk in the sandy areas and Grass Snakes can also been seen, although far less often than their four-legged cousins.

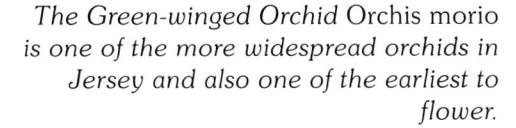

The Green-winged Orchid Orchis morio *is one of the more widespread orchids in Jersey and also one of the earliest to flower.*

Wildlife of the Channel Islands

St Ouen's Bay is also the site of the largest dune system in Jersey, Les Blanches Banques. Home to the Green Lizard, Skylark, Stonechat, Kestrel, Barn Owl and Sparrowhawk, it is best known for its plant life. The Green-winged Orchids are among the first flowers to open followed through the summer by a colourful procession of other blooms. Some, like the prickly swathes of Burnet Rose, are impossible to miss while others, like the Sand Crocus, are so tiny that you must resort to hands and knees to appreciate their delicate beauty. Over four hundred and sixty species of plant have been identified in this area including sixteen that are listed as nationally endangered in the British Red Data Book. Because of these rarities small sections are fenced off to protect the more fragile plants and to gauge the effect rabbits have on the flora. However the majority of the dunes are accessible through a network of footpaths and all are free to enjoy the natural treasures the area has in abundance.

Portelet Common is a stunning example of maritime heathland and cliffs and as such is now protected for the valuable wildlife it harbours.

Seeing Wildlife of the Channel Islands

Jersey's south-west corner is home to four more areas protected for their wildlife. Les Landes du Ouest, Les Creux Country Park, Noirmont and Portelet Common are all extensive areas of heathland with stunning granite cliffs. Colonies of Herring Gulls can be seen from the footpaths as well as Oystercatchers and nesting Shags. Gorse, Prostrate Broom, Thrift, Oxeye Daisy and Sea Campion thrive on the cliffs along with the not-altogether-popular Hottentot Fig. The sandy heathlands beyond are home to some rarer flowers such as the Autumn Squill, Sand Crocus, Dwarf Rush and the ephemeral Spotted Rockrose. Insects attracted by this wealth of flowering plants are a source of food for the Green Lizard. Dartford Warblers breed here and many migrants such as Wheatears and Whinchats can be seen in the spring and autumn movements. Lower down, in the eastern corner of St Brelade's Bay, is L'Ouaisné Common, a mixture of gorse, dune, marsh and heathland. Another stronghold of the Dartford Warbler and Green Lizard, this area is perhaps most prized for its abundant small pools which provide a breeding ground for the Agile Frog.

The mile-long walk to Seymour Tower has been described as a journey into Jersey's 'last wilderness' and lies at the heart of the Channel Islands' first Ramsar site.

Moving to the opposite, south-easterly corner of Jersey the landscape changes completely. There are no steep cliffs but instead the land slopes very gently down to the sea meeting the water with a mixture of sand, mud, shingle, boulder field and low-lying rocky reef. This variety of seashore and gradual incline combine with the huge tidal range to create a vast intertidal wilderness teeming with life. The value of this area for wildlife has been recognised by having a large proportion of it being designated under the Ramsar Convention for Wetlands of International Importance. At its most extreme the tide retreats for over two miles from the high water mark revealing a perfect landscape for low water fishing and enough rock pools to keep a marine life enthusiast absorbed for a lifetime. At high tide in winter the thousands of waders that feed in this rugged and beautiful wilderness are forced to flee to the highest rocks and many can be seen from points along this part of the coast. La Rocque Harbour and Le Hocq both provide especially good vantage points for roosts of Oystercatcher, Curlew, Grey Plover, Sanderling, Redshank, Dunlin and many other waders, which are often joined by Grey Herons and the elegant newcomers, the Little Egrets. Great Crested and Slavonian Grebes, Red-breasted Mergansers and various species of Diver can be seen, as well as Brent Geese paddling in the shallows and waiting for the tide to retreat.

In contrast to the south-east, the north coast of Jersey is formed entirely of steep cliffs interrupted only by the occasional small bay or harbour. A well-maintained footpath some sixteen miles long closely follows the intricate coastline offering fabulous views of Les Écréhous and Pierres de Lecq or Paternoster, reefs, the other Channel Islands and the coast of France. The path is lined with wildflowers from early spring when Fulmars, Shags and Gulls can also be seen on their nests. Kestrels are commonly seen over the cliff tops and this is also the hunting ground of the rarer Peregrine Falcon. Jersey's only Puffins breed near Plémont and can be seen bobbing on the sea early in the evening as they prepare to return to their burrows.

Inland there are many more miles of footpath to explore. Both Queen's Valley and Val de la Mare reservoirs have circular tracks and a wide variety of woodland and freshwater birds. The old railway line between St Aubin and La Corbière is now a four-mile-long footpath and cycle way which travels through woodland, open heath and dune. This diversity of habitat is reflected in the long list of bird species likely to be encountered but two highlights to look out for are the Great Spotted Woodpecker and the Short-toed Treecreeper. About half way along the path is a patch of pine woodland at Pont Marquet which is one of the best wild areas in Jersey to see Red Squirrels. St Catherine's Wood is another haunt of these much loved mammals and again offers public access and well maintained footpaths. A stream runs through the area and there is a small reservoir and lush water meadow. Great Spotted Woodpeckers, Jays, Short-toed Treecreepers and Sparrowhawks can frequently be seen. Spotted

St Catherine's Wood is carefully managed by the States of Jersey Environment Department. In the case of fallen trees sometimes the best policy is to leave them in place for the wealth of wildlife they attract (RP)

Foxgloves Digitalis purpurea *are just one of many wildflowers thriving along the Islands' cliff paths. Their Guernsey patois name of des cllatchets refers to the local children's game of clapping the flowers between their hands to make a popping sound.*

Wildlife of the Channel Islands

Flycatchers, Wood Warblers and Golden Orioles have occasionally been recorded here on migration.

Gorey Castle and the end of St Catherine's breakwater are the best shore-based vantage points for spotting Bottle-nosed Dolphins. Their appearance is by no means guaranteed but lucky sea watchers have been rewarded with sightings remarkably close to the coast. On a warm day at Gorey, if the dolphins fail to appear, the resident colony of Wall Lizards are less likely to disappoint. They can also be seen basking on the granite in Bouley Bay and at St Aubin's Fort.

For those with a passion for marine life, Jersey has some excellent areas for scuba diving. As with all the Channel Islands, local advice must be sought on the tidal conditions but a wide array of sea creatures can be seen from the shallows to the deeper reefs and wrecks further off shore.

Seeing Wildlife of the Channel Islands

GUERNSEY

The variety of landscape in Guernsey means that it has no shortage of fascinating wildlife, despite being the most densely populated of the Channel Islands. Steep cliffs begin close to St Peter Port on the east coast and stretch all the way along the south to Pleinmont Point in the west. A well-maintained cliff path with spectacular views of the sea follows the intricate coastline past secluded bays and tiny fishing harbours. In spring and early summer the track is lined with wild flowers and offers views of Shag, Fulmar and various species of gull on their nests. The path also passes through some beautiful woodland and pine-covered slopes occasionally offering a glimpse of a real feathered treasure, the Short-toed Treecreeper. The headlands on each of the island's southern corners are well-known to ornithologists as autumn and spring migration watch points. The rare Dartford Warbler nests among the Gorse bushes at the western point, Pleinmont, and Long-eared Owls and Sparrowhawks are known to breed here. This is also an interesting area for insect life. Look out for the Glanville Fritillary butterfly and the Blue-winged Grasshopper. Colonies of Black-backed Meadow Ant, a continental species now thought to be extinct on the British mainland, have made their home here and on other Channel Island cliff tops.

A miniature member of the lily family, the Autumn Squill Scilla autumnalis *actually begins flowering in July.*

Wildlife of the Channel Islands

About a quarter of a mile off the coast lies the tiny island of Lihou, the most westerly point in the Channel Islands. The causeway that connects it to Guernsey is revealed for up to four hours either side of low water and care must be taken to leave well before it begins to cover. (The opening times of the causeway are announced in the island's press, on local BBC Radio and the internet, as well as being displayed on site.) Owned and managed by the States of Guernsey, it is extremely valuable to local wildlife including resident and migrant birds. Over a hundred species have been recorded in the area in the past thirty years, a quarter of which are considered at risk on a national scale. The Lissory shingle bank, on the southern arm of Lihou, and the islet Lihoumel to the west are particularly important areas for nesting birds including Turnstone, Ringed Plover, Oystercatcher, Shag and various species of Gull. During their breeding season of January to August Lissory is roped off so that the nesting birds are left undisturbed.

The grassland on Lihou is home to a wide variety of maritime flowering plants. Possibly the most dramatic display is revealed in late summer when hundreds of Autumn Squill carpet the sandy turf with their delicate mauve flowers. At low water huge areas of seashore are uncovered on either side of the causeway revealing n inter-tidal paradise for rock pool explorers. There are over two hundred different species of seaweed along with countless small fishes, crabs, prawns, anemones, ormers, sponges, molluscs, starfish and sea squirts.

Just along the coast to the north of Lihou is L'Érée Shingle Bank, another extremely valuable habitat that is carefully protected for its wildlife. The plant life is particularly interesting and includes many species that have evolved to survive in this difficult environment such as Sea Kale and Yellow Horned-poppy.

The west coast of Guernsey is characterised by golden sandy beaches separated by rocky headlands. In winter the bays provide food and shelter to hundreds of overwintering waders along with Little Egrets and Brent Geese. The rocky areas uncovered on low water also provide more great places for the rock pool enthusiast. The Fort Hommet headland is a wonderful mixture of coastal and dune grassland, heath and saltmarsh. It is recognised as a Site of Nature Conservation Importance and as such has been designated as a nature reserve. The flora has been much studied, revealing many rare species such as Land Quillwort and Least Adder's-tongue in winter, the tiny Dwarf Pansy in early spring and Sea Milkwort and Sand Catchfly in mid summer. Other locally common plants include the Sand Crocus and Autumn Lady's-tresses. This rich array of plant life attracts an equally colourful collection of butterflies including the Common Blue, Gatekeeper and Meadow Brown.

Inland the south-west corner of Guernsey contains three small nature reserves. The Silbe Nature Reserve is a beautiful mixture of woodland, a pond and fields criss-

L'Estainfer and Cobo Bay on the north west coast of Guernsey.

The Silbe Nature Reserve in St Pierre du Bois is one of several protected areas managed, and often owned, by La Société Guernesiaise.

A network of small streams called douits and manmade drainage channels, darrats, ensure that the land does not become water-logged and are especially important in low-lying areas. The owners of the land through which they pass must clear them annually and they are inspected by the Guernsey authorities twice a year.

Yellow Bartsia Parentucellia viscosa *thrives in marshy areas and is one of the many flowers in Guernsey's stunning orchid fields.*

crossed by footpaths. The variety of habitats here is reflected in the diversity of its bird, insect and plant life. Closer to the coast is the marshland of La Claire Mare with its viewing hides which are open to the public. Curlew, Whimbrel, Redshank and Bar-tailed Godwit roost and feed on the open grassland in winter and the reedbeds attract migrant warblers, including the rare Aquatic Warbler. Snipe, Teal, Widgeon and Shelduck are among other species that can be seen and this is also one of the few breeding sites in Guernsey for the Reed Bunting. Nearby is the Colin Best Nature Reserve. The saltmarsh, wet 'orchid' meadow and reedbed habitats at both sites are here extremely valuable for the wildlife they attract and support. Together with L'Érée Shingle Bank, L'Érée Headland and Lihou they have been recognised as an internationally important area of wetland, becoming Guernsey's first site protected under the Ramsar Convention.

To the north-west lies the Rue des Bergers Reserve which is another large pond surrounded by reeds and overlooked by a small public bird hide. Other freshwater habitats are provided by the water-filled quarries that are scattered around Guernsey and are particularly numerous in the north of the island. They date back to the nineteenth century when millions of tons of granite were exported for building and road surfacing material. Now flooded and overgrown with willows and brambles, many of these pockets of deep water have become unofficial nature reserves. Goldfish, Carp and Rudd were introduced to some for fishing and as unofficial emigrants from garden ponds. Kingfishers sometimes stop by these small pools on their migration, occasionally staying in the island for the winter.

April, May and June are without doubt the best months of the year for wildflowers in Guernsey and, just inland from Rocquaine Bay, are some small, marshy fields at Les Vicheries and La Rue Rocheuse that reveal themselves as a botanical treasure trove in these early days of summer. The Loose-flowered Orchids and Southern Marsh-orchids stand out in a haze of purple while Heath Spotted and Common Spotted-orchids add their paler blooms against a background of lush green vegetation. Ragged Robin, Yellow Bartsia, Bugle, Lady's Smock, Lesser Spearwort and Yellow Iris are among the profusion of other wildflowers adding to this stunning display. An information board is placed on the roadside and paths are mown around the edge of the fields so that visitors can relish these wonderful areas without causing them any harm.

The largest area of freshwater in Guernsey is the reservoir in St Saviour. A two-mile long footpath follows its shores providing ample opportunities to view the birds that use both the open water and the woodlands that surround much of it. Pochard, Tufted Duck and Goldeneye are often seen in winter along with Common Sandpiper, Greenshank and Green Sandpiper which feed in the mud on the margins. Flocks of Swallows and Martins swirl above the water in summer hunting insects. Kingfishers

Rosy Garlic Allium roseum, *originally a garden plant, is one of the many wildflowers growing in the dunes around Port Soif.*

Managed by the States of Guernsey Environment Department, the Bluebell Wood above Fermain Bay is a treat for the eyes and nose at the end of April when the flowers are at their best (MG).

and Little Grebes have also been seen throughout the summer and it is hoped that they may eventually breed here. The trees provide food and nest sites for many woodland species including Chiffchaff, Spotted Flycatcher, Blackcap and Firecrest. More trees and shrubs have been planted to encourage the wildlife and boxes have been put up for tits, Barn Owls and Kestrels as well as nesting baskets for Long-eared Owls.

Guernsey's northernmost parish is home to Vale Pond, all that remains of Clos du Valle, the wetland that divided the island in two until it was drained early in the nineteenth century. Now protected as a nature reserve with its own public hide, the pond is the largest area of brackish water in Guernsey and one of the most popular bird watching sites. More than one hundred and forty species have been recorded including many interesting migrants. In winter it provides a feeding ground for the Grey Heron, Little Egret, Snipe, Lapwing and Dunlin. The regular passage waders include Whimbrel, Greenshank, Common Sandpiper, Avocet and Black-tailed Godwit. Little Ringed Plover pick at the fish larvae washed in from the sea through drainage pipes at high tide. The reeds that surround the pond offer breeding sites for Moorhen and Reed Warbler as well as roosting sites for Swallows and Sand Martins. The pond-side also has important populations of salt marsh plants such as Sea Aster, Sea Club-rush and Sea Arrowgrass.

Vale has several other excellent areas for wildlife. Le Grand Pré Reserve is another valuable stretch of reed bed and marshy grassland. The Headlands at Chouet, La Jaonneuse Bay and Fort Doyle are well-known spots for watching migrating birds. Sea-watching in north-westerly winds from these points can also be rewarding with sightings of various Shearwaters and Skuas as well as impressive numbers of Gannets and Kittiwakes. The dune grassland and scrub of L'Ancresse Common is a popular replenishing point for migrants such as Redstart, Wheatear and Whinchat. The golf course has destroyed much of the natural habitat but there are still enough areas of Gorse left to support breeding populations of Dartford Warbler and Stonechat. Kestrels, the most numerous bird of prey in Guernsey, can often be seen hovering overhead as they can above much of the island's heathland and cliff top. L'Ancresse Common is also one of the few remaining sites to support the endangered Skylark which still breeds here in small numbers. Along the coast in the south-west part of the Vale is Port Soif. Here a mixture of unspoilt grassland and scrub with a natural dune front to the sea provides several important wildlife habitats and the whole area is protected as a conservation zone. A nature trail leads inland to a small pond, home to some interesting plant species as well as newts and several types of aquatic insect. On the coast Stonechat and Linnet breed in the scrub and Skylarks build their nests in the tussocks of grass. Migrants such as Wheatears and, more rarely, Dotterel are attracted to the dunes during their spring and autumn passages. The small, stripy Pisan snails

Wildlife of the Channel Islands

cluster in their dozens on the stalks of Sea Radish and other plants. However, it is the flora here that is the greatest draw for those with an interest in natural history. Among the many commoner flowers of sandy areas, such as Sand Crocus and Autumn Lady's-tresses, are rarities such as the Pyramidal Orchid, Hound's-tongue and the stunningly beautiful Bee Orchid.

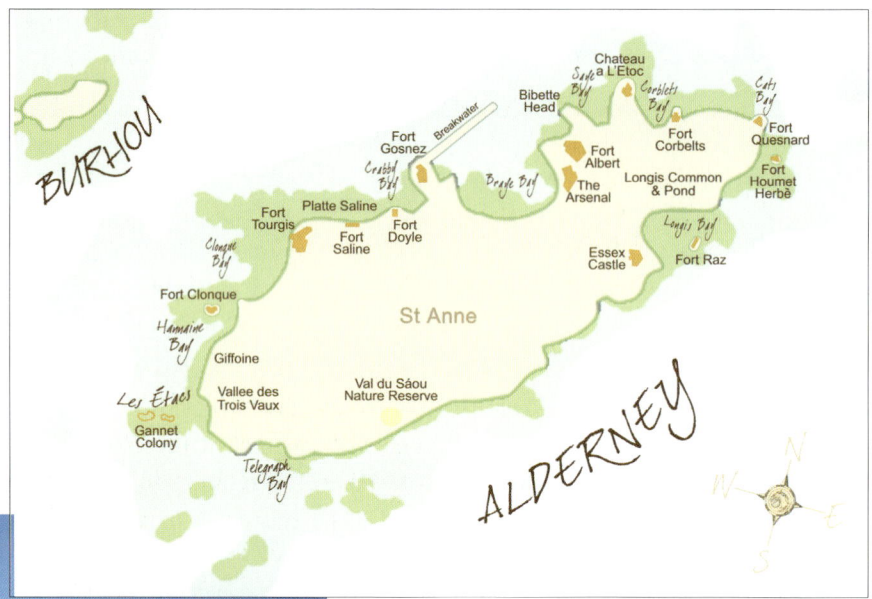

Most of Longis Common, along with the headland to the north, is now protected as Longis Nature Reserve with over three miles of footpath weaving between eight distinct habitats.

Seeing Wildlife of the Channel Islands

ALDERNEY

At just one and a half miles wide and three miles long, Alderney is the perfect size to explore on foot with no part more than an hour's gentle stroll from the capital town of St Anne. If you prefer pedal power there are bicycles available for hire. Unlike Sark and Herm cars are allowed but are easily avoided on the well-marked network of footpaths, many of which closely follow the spectacular coastline. Some of the tracks were formed by the occupying German forces when they drove their vehicles over private land in the Second World War. Much of this land is still privately owned and walkers must remember that access is a privilege rather than a right. Considerable care is needed in places, particularly around the coastline. Some of the paths run very close to the edge of the cliffs and, though the views are spectacular, there is plenty of loose rock and soil. The remains of trenches and dugouts can also be unexpectedly rediscovered around the coast and inland so walkers should take care if straying from the path.

With a wide variety of habitats ranging from rock stacks and heathland to freshwater and seashore, Alderney is a superb location for watching wildlife but is perhaps best known for its ornithology. Over two hundred and seventy species have been recorded, boosted by some unusual sightings during the autumn and spring migrations such as Rosy Starling and Red-footed Falcon. Bibette Head, Chateau à L'Étoc and the lighthouse are some of the best places to look out for migrants. Seabirds are a speciality in Alderney. Fulmars, Shags, Common Terns, Puffins, Guillemots and Razorbills can be seen from the cliff paths along with several species of Gull. Small numbers of Kittiwakes breed here too, probably their only site in the Channel Islands, but the star attraction is the Gannet colony. Two out of the three rock stacks they have colonised are just a few hundred yards offshore at Trois Vaux Bay. The Gannets arrive at the end of January and leave after their chicks have fledged in October.

Another seabird 'hot spot' is Burhou, the tiny, uninhabited island about two miles north-west of the harbour. It is owned by the States of Alderney and looked after by a warden in conjunction with the Harbour Office. It is an important breeding site for Puffins and Storm Petrels and has by far the largest colonies of both in the Channel Islands. It is also possible that Manx Shearwaters still breed on Burhou. During the breeding season, April to July, only the warden is allowed to land on the island to avoid disturbing the birds but for the rest of the year visitors can stay overnight in 'The Hut'. This basic accommodation sleeps up to eight and was built in the 1950s among the ruins of a cottage once used by fishermen and shipwrecked mariners. The remains of at least one of these ships can still be seen above the water among the treacherous rocks and reefs that surround Burhou. This is also where you are most likely to encounter Alderney's Atlantic Grey Seals. The best way to see these, and many of the seabirds, is to take to the waves aboard one of the wildlife-watching boat trips around the island. These also include a very close encounter with the Gannet colony which for me is the most spectacular sight in the Channel Islands. At the time of writing there are two boats operating these trips throughout the summer from Braye harbour.

Longis Pond was cleared by conservation volunteers at the beginning of the twenty-first century. The open water, reed beds and nearby feeding station attract a wide variety of feathered wildlife.

For wildlife that relies on freshwater the choice of accommodation is a little more restricted than for those that live by the sea. The pond at Platte Saline now dries up most summers due to its water being extracted for domestic use but there are some interesting flooded quarries and a few small marshy patches. The largest natural pond lies on the edge of Longis Common within the newly designated Nature Reserve. Thanks to the work of volunteers from the Alderney Wildlife Trust, the pond is now overlooked by a well-appointed bird hide. In summer there are Sedge, Cetti's and Reed Warblers, and Water Rails may be heard and occasionally seen. Moorhen, Coot, and Little Grebe can be seen on the water and in winter the resident ducks are joined for a while by visiting waterfowl. Kingfishers are occasionally glimpsed but Little Egrets and Grey Herons are often seen here as well as on Alderney's beaches and rocky shores. The feeding station next to the hide attracts large numbers of finches, tits and other woodland birds. Further information and another wonderful viewing point has been provided in the form of the Trust's Countryside Interpretation Centre, a refurbished World War II Radio Communications bunker. Known locally as the Wildlife Bunker it overlooks the south coast and is part of the Val du Saou Nature Reserve.

Birds of prey can be spotted almost anywhere around the island with the Kestrel being the most common. Several pairs of Peregrines now breed here as well as a pair of Common Buzzards while Merlins, Hobbies and various Harriers have regularly been reported. Strangely, Magpies are virtually never seen, although the rest of the Channel Islands have more than their fair share, and Rooks and Jays are equally rare. Woodpeckers are also absent probably due to the lack of any sizeable areas of woodland. There are some small wooded valleys which, along with the farmland and gardens, are home to many of the species common to such habitats. The cliff tops and heathland are the best places to see Linnets, Skylarks, Stonechats and Meadow Pipits with occasional sightings of the more exotic Hoopoe and Ring Ouzel. Giffoine Point, in the south-west of the island, is one of the richest areas in heathland birds including the rare and beautiful Dartford Warblers that nest in the prickly banks of Gorse. Migrants and summer visitors include Black and Common Redstarts, Wheatears, various warblers and Pied and Spotted Flycatchers. Down on the seashore the rocky bays and sandy beaches are important sites for overwintering waders such as Ringed Plover, Turnstone and Dunlin. The number of Oystercatchers also increases in the colder months as the residents are joined by those from further north.

Alderney is also a paradise for botanists with over a thousand species of flowering plant recorded in the island. Around eight hundred of those can still be found today, a remarkable level of diversity for an area of less than nine square kilometres. The list of flora includes over thirty species described in the British Red Data Book as 'nationally scarce' and several that are noted as 'endangered' or 'near threatened'. Alderney has also given its name to two plants, both of which are only found in the Channel Islands. Alderney Sea-lavender (illustrated in Chapter Three) can be found close to the water on the south-east coast among other species of Sea-lavender. The Alderney Geranium grows in the hedgerows but, like the endemic Sea-lavender, it takes a trained eye to distinguish it from the numerous other similar species. For those with an interest in lichens, look out for the last known colony in the British Isles of *Opegrapha subelevata* on the walls of the ruined Nunnery in Longis Bay.

In spring and early summer the island's cliff tops provide a display of wild flowers to dazzle all who see them, whatever their level of interest in botany. The enthusiast will delight in the tiny Sand Crocus, the ephemeral Spotted Rock-rose and the parasitic Broomrape. Both Greater and Purple Broomrape grow here in some quantity. Those

Left: The Alderney Geranium Geranium submolle *is thought to be of South American origin and is found in Jersey and Guernsey as well as Alderney. It flowers from May to September and can grow to about 80cm high scrambling among hedges.*

Below: Fort Clonque on the west coast of Alderney with the Gannet colony of Ortac rock in the background. The fort can be hired for self-catering accommodation and is surrounded, on low water, by some of the best rock pools in the island.

less well-informed can simply delight in the swathes of pink Thrift splashed yellow with Prostrate Broom and Gorse and interspersed with the cheerful faces of Ox-eye Daisies. The coastal grasslands are also home to Green-winged and Pyramidal Orchids, Small Hare's-ear, Small Restharrow and, in late summer, Autumn Lady's-tresses.

To catch a glimpse of the best-known mammal in Alderney, the 'Blonde' Hedgehog, you need to be out and about when it is; after dark. It has been estimated that at least a quarter of the island's hedgehog population have this distinctive pale colouring. Night time, particularly early evening, is also when the island's bats are most obvious. There is a significant population of Pipistrelle Bats and there may be one or two rarer species. Guided walks to see these charismatic flyers are organised by the local Bat Group.

For visitors with an interest in all things marine there is a vast rocky area exposed on low water between Fort Clonque and Fort Tourgis. The rock pools are alive with a wide variety of crabs, prawns and small fishes along with anemones and shellfish clinging to the granite. A careful search under the rocks will reveal sea squirts, Cushion Starfish, brittlestars and no end of intriguing maritime beasties. As elsewhere in the Channel Islands, keep an eye on the tide or you may risk an unplanned stay on one of the forts. Snorkelling is a wonderful way to see the marine life in its own element, particularly in the clear waters around Alderney. Take local advice on the best spots to visit and be aware of the strong tidal currents that run beyond the shelter of the bays. If total immersion is your thing then there is some wonderful scuba diving to be had around the island. Unfortunately there is no commercial dive centre but the resident dive club will sometimes take out experienced visiting divers, given enough notice.

SARK

The best way to begin your acquaintance with Sark and its wildlife is to take the daily round-the-island boat trip. Not only will you learn a little about island politics, not to mention a snatch or two of local gossip, but you will also be treated to spectacular views of the island. In May the cliffs turn an intense shade of blue as the Bluebells unfurl, followed through the summer by swathes of Thrift, Red Campion, Foxgloves and Bell Heather, to name but a few. Even in late summer the deep red brown of the Bracken as it weathers is a stunning sight. The boat will also give you the best view of the various seabirds during the breeding season. Puffins, Guillemots and Razorbills nest on the triangular shaped islet L'Étac off the south of Sark and there are even more Guillemots on the dramatic stacks called Les Autelets to the west. The well-informed skipper will also point out a Tern colony and several groups of Fulmars as well as the various species of Gull and the resident Oystercatchers. With luck the

La Grande Grève on the west side of La Coupée, the narrow isthmus linking Little Sark to the main island.

Seeing Wildlife of the Channel Islands

Peregrine Falcons may be seen and passengers have often witnessed the breathtaking spectacle of these fabulous birds of prey hunting right above their heads. Their otherworldly shrieks are impressive enough but a grandstand view of the Peregrine's aerial brilliance is something to treasure forever. The guided tour also includes a visit to one or more of Sark's caves as well as a circumnavigation of the private island, Brecqhou. If tidal and weather conditions are right you may also see a 'souffleur' blowing, a natural cascade produced when the swell traps air in the back of a sea cave causing an explosion of spray and a resounding thump. Once ashore you can spend the rest of your visit trying to rediscover the myriad secluded coves, rock formations and bathing pools that are also pointed out on the boat trip.

Sark is home to the Black Rat Rattus rattus, *now a real rarity in the British Isles and forever associated with the spread of bubonic plague. Given the right conditions each female can produce twelve litters of up to ten young each year.*

Sark is basically a rock plateau surrounded almost entirely by sheer cliffs and for visitors arriving at either of the tiny harbours the only way to the top is up Harbour Hill. There is a footpath alongside that weaves through the lovely wooded valley and emerges, as luck would have it, right next to one of the island's pubs. For the less agile, or energetic, the local tractors run a ferry service of 'toast racks' up the hill, trailers equipped with seating, for a small fee. For a truly sedate jaunt around the island join one of the horse-drawn carriage tours. The drivers have to pass a test in island history as well as equine manoeuvring before being allowed to pick up the reins unsupervised. The carriage ride will also give you an idea of the basic layout of Sark but to see more of the wildlife you need to explore on foot. Cars are not allowed on the island but take care to avoid the bicycles, which often appear unannounced and at speed around blind corners. If this is your preferred choice of transport there are several shops where you can hire bikes and various forms of trailers and extra seats for children.

Whether on foot or two wheels there is a maze of lanes and tiny tracks to explore. Some follow the rugged, fretted coastline while others lead steeply down to the tiny bays. The valley leading down to Dixcart Bay is cloaked in the island's largest area of woodland and is another wonderful site for Bluebells. The song of Robins, Chiffchaffs, Wrens, Firecrests and other woodland birds seems particularly vibrant here, maybe because they do not have to compete with aircraft noise as Sark sits under its own no-fly zone. Incidentally, Dixcart Bay is also home to the first ever sighting in the Channel Islands of the Scaly Cricket, a small brown wingless cricket that lives beneath pebbles close to the high tide mark. It is only known from a couple of locations on the British mainland and was first discovered in Sark in 1998. It has since been found in Guernsey but does not seem to live in any of the other islands even though they all have plenty of pebbly beaches.

Like all of the Channel Islands Sark lies on the migration route of many bird species and interesting sightings can be made during the spring and autumn movements. The most notable report was of a Siberian Blue Robin, the first of this species to be recorded in the whole of Europe, in Banquette valley in October 1975. Kestrels are the most common birds of prey and small numbers of Sparrowhawks and Long-eared Owls also breed in Sark.

In common with the other Channel Islands the flora of Sark is very rich and over six hundred species have been recorded. As might be expected it has a particularly high proportion of plants associated with the maritime and coastal environment. Its unique blend of wildflowers perfectly illustrates the sometimes puzzling distribution of plants in the Islands when compared to each other and the mainlands they lie between. Three-cornered Leek, for example, is abundant in Sark, and the other Islands, filling the hedgerows with masses of white, garlic-scented flowers in early spring. Originally bought from its Mediterranean home as a garden plant, it is only occasionally found in southern England yet the climate there is almost identical to that in the Channel Islands. Conversely a few of the very common British plants, such as the Harebell and Meadowsweet, are completely absent in the Islands. Sark though does have its own unique variety of Sea-lavender and has so far escaped the rampaging

Right: The footpath down to Dixcart Bay, like many tracks in Sark, is lined in early spring with Three-cornered Leek, known locally as Wild Garlic.

Below: L'Éperquerie Common looking north to the tip of the island, Bec du Nez, and the western entrance to the Boutique Caves.

swathes of Hottentot Fig, which have caused so much concern in the other Islands. The lack of intensive farming has left the fields unspoilt and their margins and hedgerows are a riot of flowers from early spring onwards. Virtually no chemicals are used on the land, which has led to Sark's particularly rich level of insect life. In summer evenings one of the most spectacular insects, the truly enormous Great Green Bush-cricket, chirrups rhythmically from the hedgerows giving the warm still nights a distinctly exotic air. Dusk also sees the emergence of the island's rat population but, if you are lucky enough to encounter one, it is worth remembering that Sark is probably the only Channel Island home of the now rare Black Rat.

L'Éperquerie Common and the other heathlands such as the Hog's Back and the Gouliot, Venus and Adonis headlands offer a wonderful variety of cliff top vegetation. Insects are attracted to the many flowers among them the rare Silver-studded Blue and Glanville Fritillary butterflies. For a more formal collection of flora the gardens at the Seigneurie are highly rated in horticultural circles.

Sark is also well known for its sea caves the longest of which are Les Boutiques caves at the northern tip of the island. The first tunnel is over sixty metres long and opens out into a lofty cavern with a view over the sea. Getting to this, and any of the other caves, involves a fairly tricky scramble down the cliffs and care must be taken not to become trapped as the tide rises. There are guide books to the caves for sale on the island but the safest way to visit them is to persuade a local to take you.

Finally, Sark has some of the most spectacular scuba diving sites in the Channel Islands with clear waters and sheer reef walls encrusted with corals, sponges and anemones. The resident dive boat skipper has excellent knowledge of local waters although the tidal surges and depth means that the diving around here is not for beginners. For those with enough experience, though, an eight knot drift along the seabed through the Gouliot Passage, the tiny gap between Sark and Brecqhou, is the thrill of a lifetime. The nearby caves are a more tranquil, though equally stunning, encounter.

HERM

If a wealth of natural history combined with stunning sea views and little other human company is your idea of paradise then Herm could be described as the perfect island. Its diminutive size means that it can be circumnavigated on foot, the only means of transport, in just a couple of hours. Yet its few square miles contain a rich mixture of landscape from undulating dunes and maritime heath to steep granite cliffs, a small mixed woodland and the famous Shell Beach.

The northern half of Herm consists almost entirely of The Common, a sandy

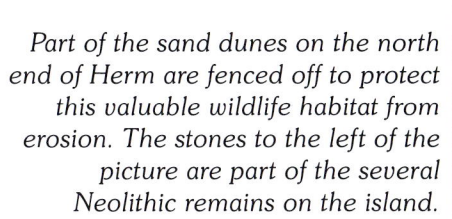

Part of the sand dunes on the north end of Herm are fenced off to protect this valuable wildlife habitat from erosion. The stones to the left of the picture are part of the several Neolithic remains on the island.

Above: Eyebright Euphrasia officinalis *is just one of the many tiny flowers on Herm Common to keep a keen botanist on hands and knees for hours.*

Right: Wildflowers such as Hogweed Heracleum sphondylium *and Red Campion* Silene dioica *thrive on the cliff tops of Herm. The famous Shell Beach can be seen in the background.*

heathland surrounded on three sides by the sea. Much of the ground is completely carpeted in Burnet Rockrose while the short turf in between contains a profusion of interesting lichens, mosses and miniature floral treasures. The smattering of Gorse bushes provide the ideal cover for migrants such as Willow Warbler, Chiffchaff and Whinchat as well as the resident Meadow Pipit, Wren, Dunnock, Robin, Blackbird and Song Thrush. In winter Redwings and Fieldfares can also be seen. Herm Common also has a number of Neolithic remains, a marshy area and a small pond surrounded by willows. This damp area is home to Gladdon, a member of the iris family, which has purple-streaked flowers to be replaced by pods of bright orangey-red berries in the autumn.

Between the heathland and the shore is a fringe of sand dunes reinforced with extra Marram Grass to protect it from erosion and dotted with Sea Holly and Yellow Horned-poppy. The almost white shingle of Shell Beach on the east sweeps all the way around the north of the island to the equally beautiful beach on the west coast. In winter both are home to flocks of Turnstone, Plover, Sanderling, Godwit and Knot and the numbers of resident Oystercatchers are swollen by visitors escaping the colder climate further north. A flock of around a hundred Brent Geese also make themselves at home between October and April.

The lane leading towards St Tugual's Chapel is flanked by a dense mixture of Pines, Giant Cypresses and Eucalyptus trees with clumps of Butcher's-broom and splashes of woodland flowers. The southern half of Herm is characterised by its sea cliffs some sixty-five metres high. The footpath follows the coastline offering uninterrupted views of Sark to the south-east and the tiny private island of Jethou to the south-west with Guernsey beyond. Puffins, Fulmars, Shags and various Gulls breed on the cliffs. In summer the Guernsey branch of the RSBP work with a local ferry company to run the Puffin Patrol, a very popular series of boat trips around Herm and Jethou especially for bird watchers. Razorbills, Guillemots and Cormorants can often be seen on fishing expeditions from their nesting sites on Les Amfroques, more commonly known as The Humps, a reef some two miles off to the north east. As with the other Channel Islands, the cliff tops of Herm are awash with wildflowers from early spring onwards. First to bloom are swathes of Sweet Violets and Primroses followed by Bluebells, Sea Campion and Thrift. By June Stonecrops, Heathers, Sheepsbit, Ox-eye Daisies, Red Campion and Foxgloves add their petals to the patchwork of colours attracting all manner of butterflies and other insects. Kestrels can be seen hovering then plunging down on prey almost anywhere over Herm and Long-eared Owls emerge to hunt after dark. House Martins, Swifts and Swallows add to the list of almost a hundred species of bird regularly seen in this tiny treasure of an island.

Japweed Sargassum muticum *is a relative newcomer which grows rapidly and reproduces very quickly. Its impact on local marine life is unknown.*

Chapter Eight

The Future

During the years I have spent photographing the wildlife of the Channel Islands and researching this book it has been impossible not to notice some of the problems facing the flora and fauna of this beautiful part of the world. It seems therefore only right to include a few words and personal thoughts on the past, present and possible future of the Islands' wildlife.

As powerful as the forces of nature are, there is one species that has influenced the natural world of the Channel Islands above all other: *Homo sapiens*. Since prehistoric man drove woolly mammoths to their deaths off what is now the south-west coast of Jersey tens of thousands of years ago, human beings have been affecting the wildlife of the Islands. The animals we have introduced for food, sport or as pets, the crops we have grown and the plants we have imported for our gardens have all had an impact, be it great or small, on the local wildlife. Even more dramatic is the way we have physically shaped the landscape. Marshes have been drained and land enclosed for agriculture and, particularly on the two larger Islands, substantial tracts of coast and countryside have disappeared beneath buildings and tarmac. Even the outline of the Islands has been altered by land reclamation, harbour walls and marinas. More insidious is the damage done to the environment by chemical pesticides and herbicides and the nitrates that seep into the water systems from artificial fertilisers.

It is tempting to look to the past, when the Islands were less built up and only seaweed was used to fertilise the land, as a halcyon period for wildlife. Yet it is worth remembering that in the nineteenth century many people owned a gun, shot and powder were inexpensive and low standards of living meant that even small birds were shot for the pot. Seabirds are less appetising but Gull, Tern and Puffin colonies were raided for their eggs. The same period saw the rise of the amateur naturalist and an age of great discovery in the natural world. However, the Victorian vogue for building up vast collections of stuffed, pressed and pickled specimens took its toll on wildlife the world over. The sorry tale of Summer Lady's-tresses, an orchid that was collected to extinction in the Channel Islands, is an extreme example of the damage caused by this passion to catalogue the natural world.

The twentieth century initially bought with it little change in attitude. A Basking

Shark stranded by the tide in Jersey's Harve des Pas bathing pool in 1951 was promptly shot, an action that today would cause a public outcry, whether the shark were a harmless plankton feeder or not. Around the same time the indiscriminate use of DDT and other persistent pesticides in the islands, as elsewhere, pushed local populations of Sparrowhawk and Peregrine Falcon to extinction. The fifties and sixties also bought a boom in building and urban development. For some people these were times of awakening environmental awareness which, over the decades, has spread through the population to a greater understanding and acceptance of conservation principles. Today, however, the Channel Islands are not without their environmental problems. Car ownership, in the Islands where vehicles are permitted, is incredibly high and the amount of rubbish produced per capita is amongst the greatest in the world. The cost of collecting and shipping suitable material to the British mainland or the Continent for processing makes recycling extremely expensive and all of the Islands struggle to dispose of their industrial and household waste. Jersey's newest reclamation site is filling up with rubble far faster than planned and Guernsey is running out of old quarries in which to dump its rubbish. Alderney retrieves the more toxic elements from its refuse before burning the rest and tipping the residue over the cliffs. In the early 1990s Jersey invested in a state-of-the-art ultraviolet sewage treatment plant which has since earned the island accolades for its bathing water quality and clean beaches. The other Channel Islands still pump much of their sewage into the sea untreated, relying on the sheer strength of the tidal currents for its dispersal. As anti-pollution regulations become increasingly demanding, all of the Islands will have to invest heavily in improving their waste management systems in the near future, whatever the financial cost.

Enhanced sewage and rubbish disposal will obviously benefit the environment but it does not address the greatest problem facing much of the Islands' wildlife; the loss or fragmentation of habitat. The coast and countryside are threatened by demands for more housing, commercial developments and recreation areas such as golf courses and motor racing tracks. Less obvious is the effect of the decline in farming within the Islands. Substantial areas which were once tended, in Alderney in particular, are now covered in bramble and bracken which smother less vigorous plants and greatly reduce an area's level of biodiversity.

There are also threats that emanate from beyond our shores and over which we have little, if any, control. The birds that rest on migration or spend the winter or summer here run the gauntlet of hunters in many of the countries they fly over, especially those that cross Africa and southern Europe. The Islands' position at the mouth of the busiest shipping lane in the world makes us vulnerable to sea-borne pollution, as the wrecking of the *Amoco Cadiz* revealed in 1978. Pair trawling further out in the Channel may pose a risk to local schools of Bottle-nosed Dolphins and our

Lampranthus *growing on the cliffs of Jersey, yet another garden escape that is thriving in the wild.*

Some small fields in Jersey have been planted with sunflowers that are delibertaely left to go to seed to provide food for wild birds, one of many conservation projects instigated by NGOs in the Channel Islands.

The Future

other marine mammals. On a larger scale, the potential for radiation pollution from Cap de la Hague reprocessing plant and Flammanville nuclear power station is a constant cause for concern along with the global issue of accelerating climate change.

The contentious question of alien species and the problems they do or do not cause in the Channel Islands is a subject large enough for a book of its own. From Slipper Limpets and Sargassum seaweed around the coast to Hottentot Figs on the cliffs and Pheasants in the open countryside, there is barely a natural habitat without some form of exotic 'invader'. Many flowers in the wild can trace their ancestors back to imported garden plants while feral ducks, cats and ferrets are all blamed for some environmental damage or other. Without doubt a few of these do cause serious problems in the natural world but it is worth remembering that some of our most familiar species, such as the Hedgehog and the Rabbit, are not native. Even the much-loved Red Squirrel was introduced by man. Perhaps it is a characteristic of islanders the world over that newcomers are more readily accepted the longer they stay and the lower the profile they keep. In the case of wildlife, being cute and furry is also an advantage.

So far this chapter makes depressing reading but I believe it is far from all bad news for the wildlife of the Channel Islands. Today the Islands' Governments have departments dedicated solely to protecting local wildlife and the habitats it relies on. Some legislation is in place to safeguard specific species while key areas have been protected as nature reserves, Sites of Scientific Interest or under the Ramsar Convention on Wetlands of International Importance. The work of these States Departments is complemented by an impressive array of non-governmental organisations from the large Sociétés and National Trusts to smaller conservation groups concerned with specific aspects of wildlife or even a single species. The members of these groups work extremely hard, and mostly without payment, to promote and protect the natural wealth of the Islands. Many are experts in their field and, without any formal training, are driven by nothing more a passion for their subject.

Between them these paid and voluntary conservationists are working to identify the problems facing local wildlife and, where possible, find a solution. The improvement in Barn Owl numbers since the introduction of specially designed nest boxes is a good example of how human intervention can prove very effective. There have also been some apparently natural changes in the Islands' bird population that have been just as welcome. Gannets were unheard of as a breeding species until the 1940s and Fulmar, Cetti's Warbler and Little Egret, all now regular breeders, are not even mentioned in Roderick Dobson's definitive book, *Birds of the Channel Islands* published in 1952. The changing distribution of these four birds, the first two spreading down from the north and the second two moving up from the south, perfectly illustrates the gradual shifts that have been happening in the natural world since long before man walked the earth. While we welcome the positive elements of such changes we need to question to what extent we are to blame for some of the losses to our local flora and fauna. Puffin numbers in the Islands have been dropping dramatically for the last twenty years yet a few hundred miles further north around the coasts of Scotland and Iceland there are hundreds of thousands. The Agile Frog is now almost impossible to find in the wild in the Channel Islands yet is plentiful enough on the nearby Continent. Some may argue that we should not worry about losing those animals and plants which survive here on the very edge of their distribution. Yet local conservationists point out that these outlying populations are often the toughest of their species and great care should be taken to find out why the edges of their distribution are contracting. Are the Puffins failing to return each spring because there are simply not enough fish in our seas to support them or are they undergoing a natural shift in their distribution? Agile Frogs are definitely suffering from the destruction and pollution of their habitat, a far from natural process. I would agree with the conservationists and add, on a personal note, that the unique blend of plants and animals from the north with those from much further south is what makes the natural history of Channel Islands so valuable and endlessly fascinating.

As with all other wildlife, be it plant or animal, the protection of its habitat is one of the most important issues facing those working to protect the Green Lizard, Lucerta bilineata.

Useful addresses & websites

Jersey

La Société Jersiaise

The Société Jersiaise was founded in 1873, has a membership of approximately 4,500 and aims to promote and encourage 'the study of the history, the archaeology, the natural history, the language and the conservation of the environment of the Island of Jersey'. It has more than 15 'sections' ranging from archaeology to zoology and produces two newsletters a year and an Annual Bulletin. The Société Jersiaise publishes books and organises lectures and guided walks which are often open to visitors. It also has a book shop, a library and a photographic archive at its headquarters in St Helier.

Société Jersiaise 7 Pier Road St Helier Jersey JE2 4XW
Tel +44 (0)1534 758314 www.societe-jersiaise.org

The National Trust for Jersey

The National Trust for Jersey was established in 1936 and is an independent and charitable organisation dedicated to preserving and safeguarding sites of historic, aesthetic and natural interest for the benefit of Jersey. The Trust owns and cares for over one hundred and thirty sites including five farms, two watermills and a rich variety of natural habitat such as woodland, heath, meadow, farmland and wetland. Many of these sites are open to the public and guided walks and tours are often available.

National Trust for Jersey The Elms La Chève Rue St Mary Jersey JE3 3EN
Tel + 44 (0)1534 483193 www.nationaltrustjersey.org.je

States of Jersey Environment Department

The Environment Department is part of the States of Jersey Environment and Public Services Committee. It exists to implement the mandate of the Committee as the organisation with strategic and co-ordinating responsibility for environmental policy in Jersey.

Environment Department Howard Davis Farm Trinity Jersey JE4 8UF
Tel +44 (0)1534 866200 www.env.gov.je

Jersey Tourism Liberation Square St Helier Jersey JE1 1BB
Tel +44 (0)1534 500 700 www.jersey.com

Jersey Birds web site **www.jerseybirds.co.uk**

Guernsey

La Société Guernesiaise
La Société Guernesiaise is Guernsey's local research, natural history and conservation organisation. It was founded in 1882 and its objects are 'the study of all aspects of natural science and local research within the Bailiwick of Guernsey, including archaeology, history, genealogy, folklore, language, geography and geology, and the conservation of fauna and flora, including marine fauna and flora, and of buildings, objects and features of historic interest.' It publishes a newsletter three times a year, an annual Report and Transactions and holds meetings, lectures and guided visits around Guernsey and the smaller islands. La Société Guernesiaise also publishes books and owns or manages the majority of the nature reserves in the island.

La Société Guernesiaise Candie Gardens St Peter Port Guernsey GY1 1UG
Tel +44 (0)1481 725093 www.societe.org.gg

The National Trust of Guernsey
The Trust was founded in 1960 and its aims are 'to preserve and enhance the Island's natural beauty, its historic buildings and its heritage'. A registered charity, it is purely an island organisation with its own constitution and funds. It is wholly independent and relies for its finances entirely on gifts, legacies, members' subscriptions and annual fund-raising. Several large areas of land with beautiful walks are owned and maintained by the Trust with well-kept paths and seats at strategic viewing points, open for everyone's enjoyment at all times.

The National Trust of Guernsey 26 Cornet Street St Peter Port
Guernsey GY1 1LF
Tel +44 (0)1481 728451 www.nationaltrust-gsy.org.gg

The States of Guernsey Environment Department
The Environment Department of the States of Guernsey is responsible for the island's environmental policy and management of States and Crown. This includes maintaining the coastal paths, nature trails and conservation areas such as Lihou Island. The Department decides land use policy and controls development, conservation and heritage protection, public transport, traffic and road related issues as well as waste management, recycling and energy conservation initiatives.

Environment Department Sir Charles Frossard House La Charroterie St Peter Port Guernsey GY1 1FH
Tel + 44(0)1481 717000 www.gov.gg

Useful Addresses and websites

Visit Guernsey PO Box 23 St Peter Port Guernsey GY1 3AN
Tel +44 (0)1481 723552 www.guernseytouristboard.com

Alderney

Alderney Wildlife Trust
The Alderney Wildlife Trust was launched in 2002 with the stated aim to 'protect Alderney's wildlife and countryside and to ensure Alderney retains its unique nature'. Since then the Trust has established a nature reserve and bird hide at Longis Pond and is working with the local government on a wide programme of environmental management and ecological resources issues. Alderney Wildlife Trust publishes its own newsletters and runs an extensive programme of conservation projects, walks, lectures and even guided snorkelling expeditions for its members and visitors.

Alderney Wildlife Trust Wildlife/Tourism Information Centre Victoria Street
Alderney GY9 3AA
Tel +44 (0)1481 822935 www.alderneywildlife.org

Alderney Tourism Information Centre Victoria Street
Alderney GY9 3AA
Tel +44 (0)1481 822935 www.alderney.gov.gg

Burhou Island web site
www.burhou.com

Sark

Sark Tourism Harbour Hill Sark Channel Islands GY9 0SB
Tel +44 (0)1481 832345 www.sark-tourism.com

Herm

Herm Island Tourism Enquiries Guernsey GY1 3HR
Tel +44 (0)1481 722377 www.herm-island.com

South Coast, Guernsey

Bibliography

The following publications have been invaluable in the preparation of this book. While some are rather specialised, this list provides a wealth of information for those wishing to delve deeper into the natural history of the Channel Islands.

Allen, A (1993) *Wildflowers of Sark, Field Companion*, Ann Allan & Barbara Hilton

d'Aguilar, J, Dommanget, J & Préchac, R (1986) *A Field Guide to the Dragonflies of Britain & Europe*, Collins

Arnold, E N & Burton, J A (1978) *A Field Guide to the Reptiles & Amphibians of Britain & Europe*, Collins

Bichard, J D & McClintock, D (1975) *Wildflowers of the Channel Islands*, Chatto & Windus

Boddye, E (1996) *Walks on Little Sark*, Guernsey Press

Bonnard, B & Dr J, (1995) *A Natural History of Guernsey, Alderney, Sark & Herm*, Guernsey Press

Bonnard, B (1993) *Channel Island Plant Lore*, Guernsey Press

Bristowe, W S (1958) *The World of Spiders*, Collins (New Naturalist)

Caldwell, G ed. (1994) *Wildflowers of the Baliwick of Guernsey*, La Société Guernesiaise, Guernsey

Campbell, A (1994) *Seashore & Shallow Seas of Britain & Europe*, Hamlyn

Cooper, A (1992) *Secret Nature of the Channel Shore*, BBC Books

Daly, S (1998) *Marine Life of the Channel Islands*, TFH Kingdom Books

Dipper, Dr F (2001) *British Sea Fishes*, Underwater World Publications

Double, P (1996) *Wild Island, Jersey Nature Year*, Seaflower Books

Feltwell, Dr John (2001) *Field Guide to Butterflies & Other Insects*, Reader's Digest

Jee, N (1967) *Guernsey's Natural History*, Guernsey Press Co. Ltd

Jee, N (1997) *Guernsey Country Diary*, Seaflower Books

Kendrick, J S (1969) *Fifty Seashells From Herm Island*, Guernsey Press Co. Ltd and the Author

Le Sueur, F (1976) *A Natural History of Jersey*, Phillimore

Le Sueur, F (1984) *Flora of Jersey*, Société Jersiaise

Le Sueur, F (1980) *Some Cetti's Warbler Breeding Observations*, Bird Study 27:249-253, The Journal of the British Trust for Ornithology.

Lellák, J (1975) *Shells of Britain and Europe*, Hamlyn

Bibliography

McClintock, D (1975) *The Wildflowers of Guernsey,* Collins

Rowe, G (1995) *Common Life on the Seashore of the Channel Islands,* La Société Guernesiaise

Stenitford, M (1999) *The Birdwatchers' Jersey*, States of Jersey Environmental Services Unit

Vernon, P K (1997) *Important Sites for Birds in the Channel Islands, Including Recognised Important Bird Areas,* La Société Guernesiaise, Guernsey

Guernsey Coastal Walks & Nature Trails (2000) States of Guernsey Board of Administration, Environment Services

Trees in Jersey (1997) The Jersey Association of the Men of the Trees

Acknowledgements

I would like to thank the following Channel Islanders for their help in writing this book. Many are experts in their field and all gave generously of their knowledge and encouragement. Lesley Bailey, Kate Balcam, Brian Bonnard, Robert Burrow, Grif Caldwell, Brian De Carteret, Jennifer Cochrane, Pat Costen, Charles David, Peter Double, Michael Dryden, Roland Gauvain, Martin Gavet, Jen Gilmour, George Guille, Therese Holley, Fay Holroyd, Andy Leaman, Julia Meldrum, Jan Le Noury and Michael Stentiford MBE. Thanks also to the photographers listed below for the use of their beautiful images and to Val Le Sueur for the graphics. Special thanks are due to Roger and Margaret Long for their invaluable advice and support and for all their hard work as copy editors. Finally to Mark Neal who has carried my camera equipment for miles, taken me to the remotest parts of these Islands and without whom this book could not have been written.

All photographs are by Sue Daly except those indicated by the photographers initials as listed below.

AC – Andrew Cooper

MD – Mick Dryden

MG – Martin Gavet

FG – Frank Greenaway

JED – Jersey Environment Dept

RL – Roger Long

JM – Julia Meldrum

RP - Richard Perchard

JP – Jean Powell

TR – Tony Rive

CW – Chris Wood

SoA – States of Alderney

Sunset over St. Aubin's Bay, Jersey

Index

(Illustrations in bold)

Adonis Headland 198
Alderney 12, 189-193
Alderney Race **27**
Alexanders 146
Agriculture 17-18, 137-140
Amfroques, Les **59**
Amphibians 162
L'Ancresse Common 187
Anemones
    Beadlet **103**
    Colonial **118**
    Imperial **123**
    Jewel **118**, 119
    Nocturnal **128**
    Snakelocks **104**, 105, **119**
Ânes, Les 163
Ant, Black-backed Meadow 181
Ant-lion 84, **85**
Les Autelets **50**, 51, 193

Bats **155**, 193
Bee, Scilly **33**, 33-34
Bibette Head 189
Blanches Banques, Les **76**, 77, 176
Blenny
    Black-face **126**
    Tompot **99**, 100
Bluebells **23**, 24, **169**, **186**
Bouley Bay 180
Boutique Caves 198
Bracken 24
Branchage 147
Brecqhou 13, **31**, 70, 195
Bréhon Tower **52**, 53
Brent Goose 65-67, **66**
Broom, Prostrate **25**, 26
Broomrape **20**, 26
Burhou 13, 189-190
Burnet Rose **77**, 78, 176
Burnet moth, Five-spot **82**
Bush-cricket, Great Green 84

Buttercup, Jersey **146**
Buzzard, Common 191
Cabot 99
Campion
    Sea **21**, 22
    Red **200**
Casquets Reef 13, **41**, 42
Cattle **139**, 140
Cetaceans 129-131
Chouet 187
La Claire Mare 185
Climate 15-16
Clingfish, Shore **100**
Cobo Bay **183**
Cockles **63**, 64
Colin Best Nature Reserve 185
Comma butterfly **140**
Common Blue butterfly **83**
Compass Jellyfish **115**
Corals 121-122
    Red Fingers **112**, **121**
    Sea Fan **2**, **112**, **117**
    Sunset **121**
Coralline Algae **94**, 95
Cormorant 55, **61**
Corn Marigold **17**
Couch Grass 77
Cowrie **63**, 64
Crabs
    Chancre 97, **98**
    Edible 97, **98**
    Hermit **95**
    Porcelain **101**, 102
    Scorpion Spider **123**
    Shore **95**, 96
    Spider 127
    Velvet Swimming **97**
Crapaud 163
Les Creux Country Park 177
Cricket
    Field 84,

217

Index

Mole 160, **161**
Scaly 196
Crocus, Sand 15, **24**, 25
Cudweed, Jersey **31**, 32
Curlew 69
Cushion Star **101**, 102
Cuttlefish 113-115, **114**

Daffodils **138**, 139
Damselflies 160
　　Common Blue **159**
　　Southern Emerald **160**
Darrats **184**
Dixcart **169**, 196, **197**
Dodder **26**
Dogfish egg **117**
Dog-violet **145**
Dolphins 129-131
　　Bottled-nosed **130**, 171, 204
Douits **184**
Dove, Turtle **152**
Dragonet **126**, 127
Dragonflies 160, 174
Duck, Tufted **165**
Dunlin **68**
Dutch Elm Disease 152

Echium, Giant **15**
Les Écréhous **8**, **53**, **54**, 178
Eel
　　Grass 65, **66**, 113
　　Conger **133**
　　Sand 113
Egret, Little 69, **109**, 110, 207
L'Éperquerie Common **197**, 198
L'Érée Shingle Bank 182, 185
L'Estainfer **183**
L'Étac (Sark) **48**, 50, 193
Les Étacs (Alderney) **42**, 43
Eyebright **200**

Falcon, Peregrine **37**, 38-39, 50, 204
Falle, Phillipe 133
Fieldfare 30
Fern, Jersey **147**, 149
Fort Clonque **192**, 193

Fort Doyle 187
Fort Hommet 182
Fort Raz **27**
Fort Tourgis 193
Fox, Red 141
Foxglove **179**
Fragrant Evening-primrose **78**
Frogs 161
　　Agile **161**, 208
　　Common 161
Fulmar **49**, 50, 207
Furze 26

Gannet **42**, **43**, 42-44, 189, 207
Garden Rocks (Alderney) **42**, 43
Garlic, Rosy **186**
Le Gastelois, Alphonse 54
Gatekeeper butterfly 34
Geranium, Alderney **192**
Glanville Fritillary butterfly **35**
Goby, Giant **89**
Golden Oriole 30
Gorse 17, 26-28, **27**
Gouliot Caves **103**, 198
Gouliot Passage 103, 198
La Grand Pré Reserve 187
La Grande Grève **194**
Grasshopper, Blue-winged **83**, 84
Grebe, Great Crested **109**
Green Hairstreak butterfly 34
La Grève de la Ville 170
Guernsey 12, 181-188
Guernsey Lily 18
Guillemot 50, **51**, 52
Gulf Stream 15
Gulls
　　Great Black-backed **45**, 46, 50, 141
　　Herring 50, **55**, 55-56
Gurnard, Tub **127**, 128-129

Hare's-tale Grass **81**
Harrier, Marsh **168**
Heather **31**, 173
Hedgehog, Blonde **141**, 142, 193
Herm **62**, **171**, 198-201, **199**
Herm Common 201

218

Index

Heron **164**, 165
Le Hocq 178
Hog's Back 198
Hogweed **200**
Hottentot Fig 18, **22**, 22-23, 76, 207
The Humps **59**
Hurd Deep 113
Hydroid, Oaten-pipe 132

Iris, Yellow **156**

La Jaonneuse Bay 187
Japweed 93, **202**
Jersey 11, 173-180
Jethou 12, **13**
John Dory **128**, 129

Kelp 90
Kempt Tower 174
Kestrel 19, **37**, 38, 144
Kingfisher **164**, 165

Lady's-tresses 159, 203
Lampranthus **205**
Les Landes 173
Les Landes du Ouest 177
Leek, Wild **62**
Lapwing **30**, 168, 174, 175
Latticed Stinkhorn **153**
Lichen 16, **17**, **21**, 22
Lihou 13, 90, 182, 185
Lihoumel **182**
Limpet 63, **64**, 65, 89-90
Limpet, Blue-rayed 90
Linnet 28
Lissory Shingle Bank 182
Lizards
    Green 84-85, **85**, **208**
    Wall 149, **150**
Lobster 97-99, **98**, 128
Longis Common 163, **188**
Longis Pond 190, **191**
Low water fishing **107**, 108
Lugworm casts **67**
Lumpsucker **124**, 125

Magpie 14
Mallard 165
La Mare au Seigneur 163, 175
Marram Grass **76,** 77, 78
Martins 166
Meadow Brown butterfly 34
Mermaid's Purse **117**
Mexican Fleabane **148**, 149
La Mielle de Morville 174
Les Minquiers 13, **40**, **56**, 57
Moles 14
Mice 14, 142, 144
Mussel **64**, 65, 109

Navelwort **147**
Necklace Shell **63**, 64
Newts 162
Le Noir Pré 174
Noirmont 177
Nudibranchs **122**, **123**, 124

Oar-weed 90
Octopus 115
Opegrapha subelevata 191
Orange Tip butterfly **140**
Orchards 137
Orchid fields, Guernsey 185
Orchid fields, Jersey 174-175
Orchids 80-82, 157-159
    Bee **80**, 81
    Common Spotted- 159
    Early Purple 81
    Green-winged 81, **175,** 176
    Heath Spotted- **158**, 159
    Jersey **136**, 157, 159
    Lizard **80**, 81-82
    Pyramidal **81**, 82
    Southern Marsh- **158**, 159
Ormer **106**, 107
Ortac 42
L'Ouaisne Common 177
Owl, Barn **143**, 144, 207
Owl, Long-eared 144
Owl, Short-eared 144
Oyster Drill **63**, 64
Oyster farming **108**, 109

Index

Oystercatcher 19, **60**, 69

Painted Lady butterfly 34
Pansy, Dwarf 78
Partridges 145
Paternosters 178
Periwinkles **63**, 64, 89-90
Petrel, Storm 46, **47**
Pheasant **145**, 144, 207
Pierres de Lecq 178
Pinel, Phillipe 54
Pipefish, Worm 100
Pipit, Meadow 29, 173, 175
Platte Saline 163, 190
Plémont 178
Pleinmont Point **181**
Plover, Ringed **68**
Pont Marquet 178
Poppy
    Common **137**
    Yellow Horned- **70**
Port Soif 187-188
Portelet Common **176**, 177
Potatoes 138
Pouting **132**
Prawn
    Anemone 105, **119**
    Common 96
Primrose **39**
Puffin **44**, 45-46, 50, 208

Queen's Valley 178

Rabbit 55, 141, 207
Ragged Robin **157**, 175
Rats
    Black 142, **195**
    Brown 142
Razor Shell 63, **64**, 65
Razorbill **49**, 50, 51
Red Admiral butterfly 34
Red Valerian **148**, 149
Redwing 30
Ring Ouzel 30
Robin, Siberian Blue 196
La Rocco Tower **173**

Rock-rose, Spotted **25**
La Rocque Harbour 178
Rough Star Thistle 78, **79**, 174
Rue des Bergers Reserve 185
La Rue Rocheuse 185

St Catherine's Breakwater 180
St Catherine's Wood 178, **179**
St Ouen's Bay 63, 77, **111**, **173**, **174**
St Ouen's Pond 163, 168, 175
St Peter Port Daisy 148**, 149**
St Saviour's Reservoir 185
Saddle Oyster **63**, 64
Samphire, Rock 22, 70, **71**
Sand Dunes 73-77, **76**, **199**
Sanderling 69
Sark 12, 99, 142, 193-198
Scallops
    Great **63**, 64, **116**, 118
    Queen **63**, 64
Scuba diving 180, 193, 198
Sea Beet 22, 57, 70
Sea Bindweed **74**, 76
Sea Hare 105, **106**
Sea Holly 76, **82**
Sea Ivory **17**
Sea Kale 70, **71**
Sea Sandwort 73, **74**
Sea shells 63, **64**, 65
Sea Spleenwort **22**
Sea Spurge **76**
Sea Squirts 102
Seahorse, Short-snouted **134-135**
Seal, Atlantic Grey 47**, 48**
Sea-lavender, Alderney **75**, 76
Seymour Tower **86**, **177**
Shag **50**, **55,** 57**,** 58
Shanny **99**, 100
Shark, Basking **131**, 203
Sheep's-bit **23**
Shell Beach 62**, 63, 201**
Shipwrecks 131-133, **132**
Shrews 14, **72**, 73, **143**, 144
Silbe Nature Reserve 182, **183**
Silver-studded Blue butterfly **34**, 35
Skipper butterflies **82**, 84

Index

Skylark **29**, 173, 175
Slipper Limpet **92**, 93, 207
Slow Worm **36**, 37
Snail, Pisan 70, **72**, 73
Snake, Grass **36**, 175
Souffleur 195
Sparrowhawk 153, 204
Speckled Wood butterfly **152**
Spider, Wasp **32**, 33
Sponge, Shredded Carrot **94**, 95
Squat Lobster 100, 102
Squill, Autumn **181**
Squirrel, Red **154**, 207
Star Squirt **102**
Starfish, Spiny **117**, 118
Stonechat 28, 173
Swallow 166, 175
Swallowtail butterfly **18**
Swans 166
Swifts 166

Tamarisk 151
Tern, Common **52**, 53, 55
Three-cornered Leek 18, **145**, 146
Thrift **21**, 22, 76
Thrift, Jersey **15, 22,** 75, **76**
Thyme, Wild **173**
Tides 87-88
Tiger Moth, Jersey **35**, 36
Toads 162, **163, 174**
Toadflax, Ivy-leaved **148**, 149
Tomatoes 138-139
Topshells
    Painted **63**, 64
    Pennant's 90, **91**
    Purple **63**, 64, 90
    Turban **63**, 64
Trees **150**, 151-152
Tree Lupin 78, **79**, 174
Treecreeper, Short-toed 153
Tree-mallow **56**, 57
Triggerfish **129**

Trois Vaux Bay 189
Tufted Duck **165**
Turnstone 69
Tusk Shell **63**, 64

Val de la Mare Reservoir 178
Val du Saou Nature Reserve 191
Vale Pond **163, 187**
Venus Pool **88**, 198
Les Vicheries **185**
Violet, Sweet **146**
Viper's-bugloss, Purple **31**, 32
Voles **13**, 14, 142, 144
Vraic **90**
Vraitcheurs **92**

Wall Pennywort **147**, 149
Wakame 93
Warblers 167
    Cetti's **167**, 175, 207
    Dartford **27**, 28, 173
    Reed **166**, 167, 175
Wentletrap, Common **63**, 64
Whale, Long-finned Pilot 129, **130**, 171
Wheatear **29**
Whelks
    Common **104**, 105
    Dog **63**, 64, 105
    Netted Dog- **63**, 64
Whitethroat 28
Woodpecker, Great Spotted 153
Worms
    Green Leaf (eggs) **104**, 105
    Mint Sauce **67**, 68
Wrack 89-90
Wrasse
    Corkwing 125
    Cuckoo **120**

Yellow Bartsia **184**
Yellow Rattle **156**

SEAFLOWER BOOKS

Our first title, JERSEY RAMBLES, was published in 1992. Since then we have published many more, on all aspects of the Channel Islands, but with an emphasis on Jersey.

WILDLIFE OF THE CHANNEL ISLANDS is our twenty-seventh book. Three titles are now out of print but the remaining twenty-three are still available and are featured on the following two pages.

Our books may be obtained through your local bookshop or direct from the publisher, post-free, on receipt of net price.

Contact SEAFLOWER BOOKS at
16A New St John's Road
St Helier   Jersey
JE2 3LD

e-mail: roger.jones.ex-librisbooks.co.uk
www.ex-librisbooks.co.uk

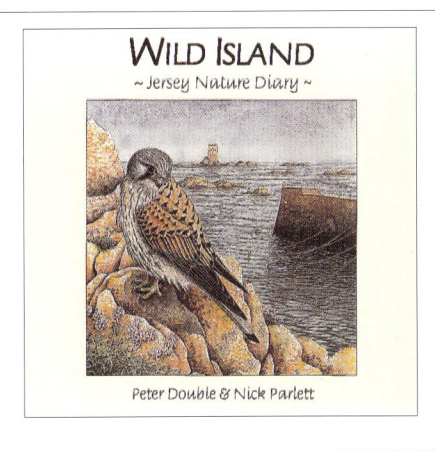

WILD ISLAND
~ Jersey Nature Diary ~

Peter Double & Nick Parlett

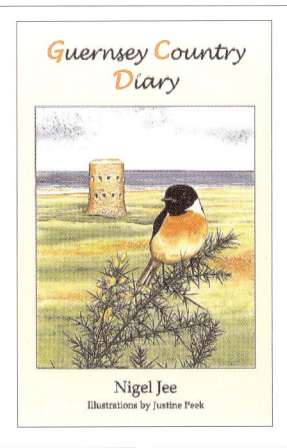

Guernsey Country Diary

Nigel Jee
Illustrations by Justine Peek

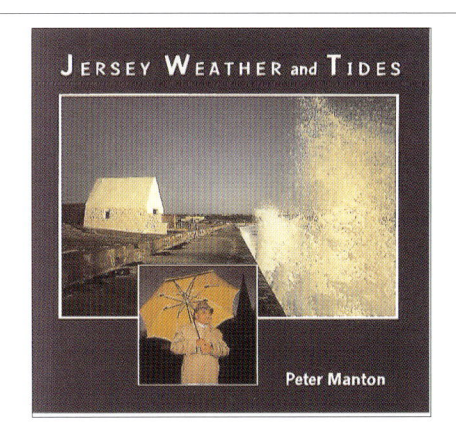

JERSEY WEATHER and TIDES

Peter Manton

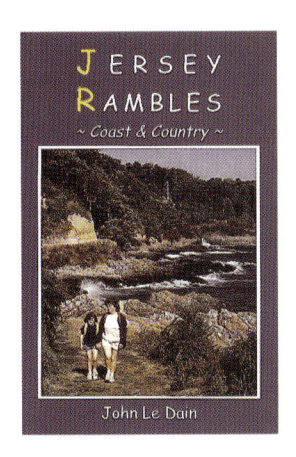

JERSEY RAMBLES
~ Coast & Country ~

John Le Dain

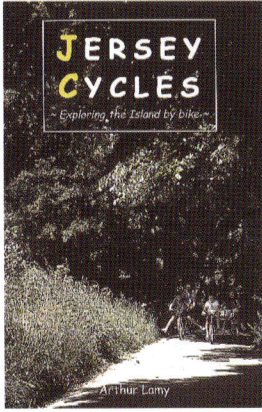

JERSEY CYCLES
~ Exploring the Island by bike ~

Arthur Lamy

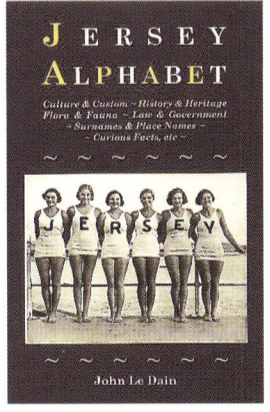

JERSEY ALPHABET
Culture & Custom ~ History & Heritage
Flora & Fauna ~ Law & Government
~ Surnames & Place Names ~
~ Curious Facts, etc ~

John Le Dain

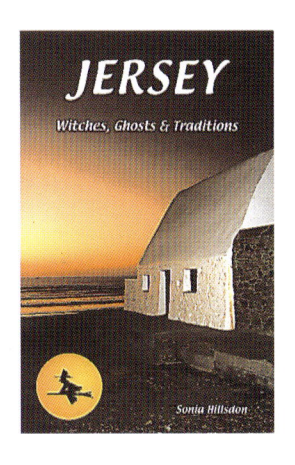

JERSEY
Witches, Ghosts & Traditions

Sonia Hillsdon

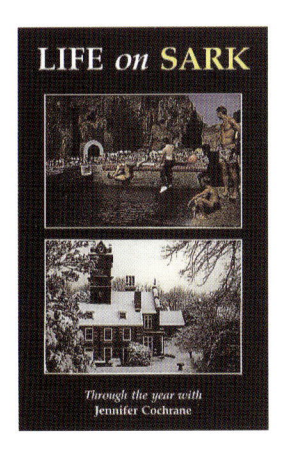

LIFE on SARK

Through the year with
Jennifer Cochrane

JERSEY
Not quite British

The Rural History of a Singular People

The Sea was their Fortune
A Maritime History
of the Channel Islands

Roy McLoughlin

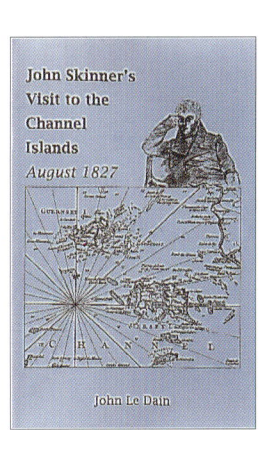

John Skinner's Visit to the Channel Islands
August 1827

John Le Dain

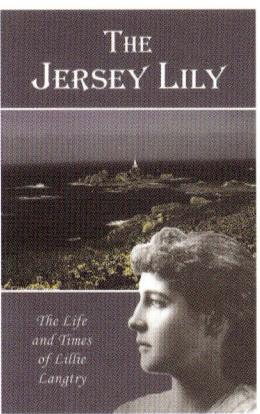

THE JERSEY LILY

The Life
and Times
of Lillie
Langtry

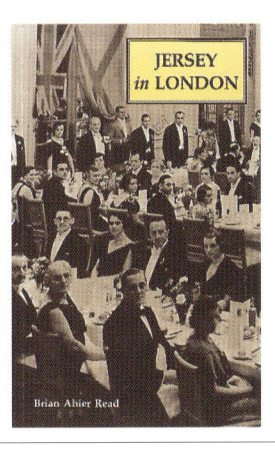

JERSEY in LONDON

Brian Abier Read

ISLAND KITCHEN
A Book of Seasonal Cookery from the Channel Islands

~ Marguerite Paul ~

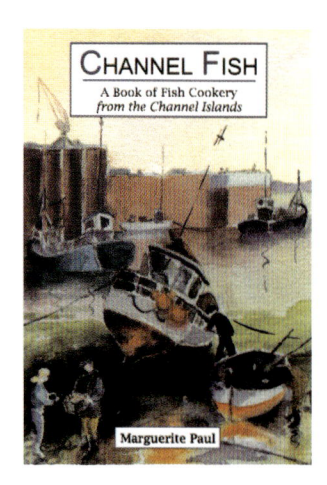

CHANNEL FISH
A Book of Fish Cookery from the Channel Islands

Marguerite Paul

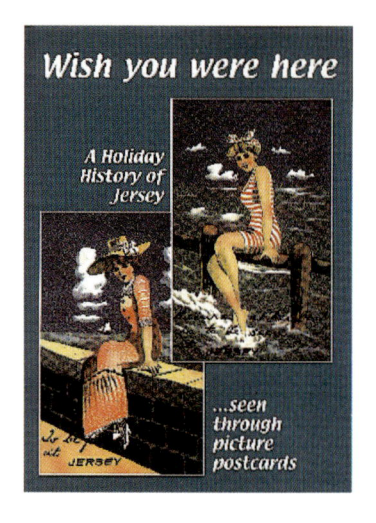

Wish you were here
A Holiday History of Jersey

...seen through picture postcards

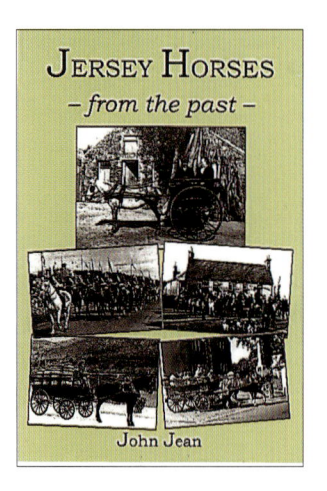

JERSEY HORSES
– from the past –

John Jean

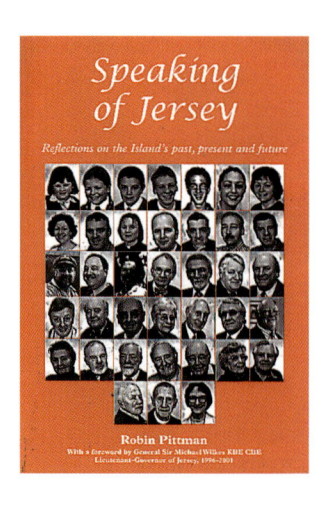

Speaking of Jersey
Reflections on the Island's past, present and future

Robin Pittman
With a foreword by General Sir Michael Wilkes KBE CBE
Lieutenant-Governor of Jersey, 1996-2001

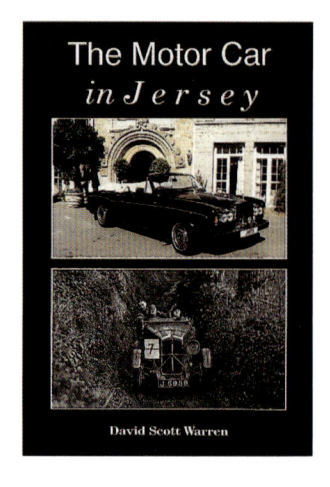

The Motor Car in Jersey

David Scott Warren

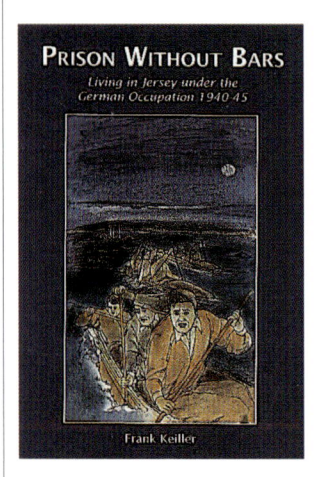

PRISON WITHOUT BARS
Living in Jersey under the German Occupation 1940-45

Frank Keiller

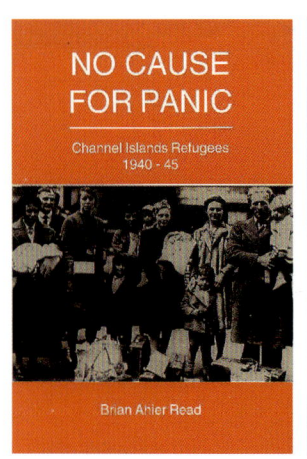

NO CAUSE FOR PANIC
Channel Islands Refugees 1940 - 45

Brian Ahier Read

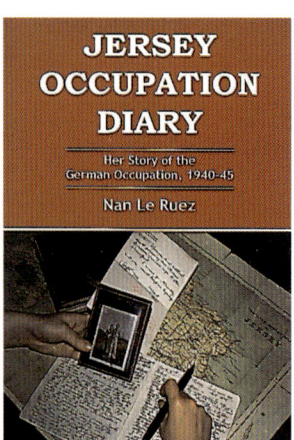

JERSEY OCCUPATION DIARY
Her Story of the German Occupation, 1940-45

Nan Le Ruez

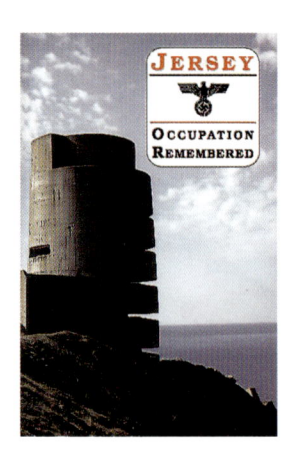

JERSEY
OCCUPATION REMEMBERED